To my n
Jeff Martin,

I hope you enjoy taking a ride on my Journey of Life.

Love to you, your family and friends,

Michael S. Olesiuend

774-454-1612

Don't TAKE IT FOR Granted

THE JOURNEY WITHIN

Michael G. Oliveira

Don't Take It For Granted
The Journey Within
Michael G. Oliveira

ISBN (Print Edition): 979-8-35091-123-7
ISBN (eBook Edition): 979-8-35091-124-4

© 2023. All rights reserved. No part of this publication may be reproduced, distributed, or transmitted in any form or by any means, including photocopying, recording, or other electronic or mechanical methods, without the prior written permission of the publisher, except in the case of brief quotations embodied in critical reviews and certain other noncommercial uses permitted by copyright law.

CONTENTS

Introduction ... 1

Chapter One *Phase One: Growing Up* ... 7

Chapter Two *Springfield College* ... 15

Chapter Three *Phase Two: Exploring Adulthood* ... 27

Chapter Four *Career and Relationship* ... 33

Chapter Five *Michael meets Nancy* ... 41

Chapter Six *The Big Move* ... 53

Chapter Seven *Phase Three: Learning to Mature* ... 69

Chapter Eight *Caregiving 101* ... 81

Chapter Nine *Phase Four: Learning from Grief* ... 97

Acknowledgements ... 115

Special Moments of Love and Wisdom ... 125

The Way We Were ... 133

Words from Michael ... 143

INTRODUCTION

IT WAS THE MORNING OF AUGUST 25, 2006, NANCY AND I were spending time at the Martha's Vineyard family cottage. We got up to enjoy our morning coffee and then took a power walk around Oak Bluffs. It was a beautiful morning with plans to meet friends for lunch and a gathering at the cottage later. Nancy and I prepared appetizers for that afternoon, however, first, we met Ed and Mary Ann for lunch at Nancy's Restaurant in Oak Bluffs. It was going to be a perfect afternoon. We met at the restaurant and enjoyed our lunch. I received a call from our other friends Brian and Cathy who were on the Vineyard for the day. At that moment Nancy suddenly got up, then quickly sat down and said "I don't feel very well". At 1:48 pm she collapsed, and we rushed her to the hospital on the island. Before the EMT's and ambulance left, I recall sitting in the passenger's seat in the ambulance observing them assess Nancy's condition. I was looking out over Church's Pier, where Nancy and I spent much of our time. I was experiencing a strong feeling that our lives were going to change forever.

My name is Michael, however, I have a number of nicknames which will become familiar as the story unfolds. I am of Cape Verdean descent from New Bedford, Massachusetts. I grew up with my sister, Gail and our parents near the south end of the city, where I attended kindergarten through high school. I am writing this book for a number of reasons. One of them being therapeutic, by journaling a life, or in this case, two lives and how in a moment, everything can change. I feel it to be important to spend time reflecting upon the journey within, to learn more about myself and how I became the man I am today. Putting it down on paper helps me understand the choices I made, how they benefited me and how they affected me. I also believe my journey could benefit others, particularly caregivers and those experiencing grief, or those who have lost hope. We all know life has ups and downs. I have come to believe having a positive attitude can change us for the better. Sometimes it's hard to see the positivity in a situation, but positivity and hope requires strength. I know it worked for me sometimes and I saw positivity in Nancy until the day she passed.

There is always more to learn with an open mind. I like to approach each new day eager to learn something more about myself and the world around me. This has been a mindset in the past and I hope I continue to feel curious about life in the future. I try to focus on thoughts and activities that will help me through the harder times. This might sound insignificant but, for me, living moment to moment gave me hope. I found having faith was, and will be helpful through difficult times in life.

Discipline for me was and still is the key to being successful in life by pacing myself as I approach problems or lifestyle changes. If I am going 100 miles an hour with no direction, it can cause a major slowdown in my growth. I had to learn I was human and mistakes will be made. Perfection is a high bar to set for oneself. The other important piece, which was and still is a challenge, is to try not to judge myself too harshly. I try to change perspectives before making choices, trying to make sure to do the best in a situation. In general, I try my best to move forward, seek purpose, experience each day and to help someone else in the process. It is rewarding and I enjoy a sense of accomplishment. It is a helpful process for staying out of a rut which could easily lead to depression.

I have come to believe that spirit, mind, and body are also three keys to a successful life. They work hand in hand. It is a challenge, however, keeping all three healthy, but the rewards of working on these each day offer positive benefits. Caregivers and those who are grieving are much more susceptible to a struggle while keeping themselves emotionally, mentally and physically healthy. How I accomplished this was by participating in physical activities. I would also spend quiet time simply thinking, meditating, and reading.

I thought then and still think about the positive impact of tolerance, self-reflection, resilience and inclusiveness. A positive attitude helped me resist the temptation to quit when things got rough. Obviously, any task needs to be reasonable. I don't believe there is anyone who wants to be set up for failure. As I continue this journey of writing, I will dig deeper into my own learning and hope I can assist in helping others on their journey of caregiving and grief.

After having time to self-reflect, I believe life, if you are lucky, is separated into four phases that overlap at times. Phases are fluid and individual experiences are different for everyone.

Phase One are the "growing up" years from birth to college graduation or the twenty's. Hopefully, if there is luck on your side you have a good environment to thrive in. I consider myself lucky in that respect, my family was always supportive. If not, do your best to seek out mentors in your life such as a school counselor, coach, teacher or relative. If you're lucky, surround yourself with good friends who you can trust to point you in the right direction. Life is a classroom and with a good foundation in this classroom on earth, you have a running start to be successful in life. Earth's classroom is about all living things in the physical world being here for a purpose. It is about learning what our individual purpose is, here on earth. Everything takes time and as I came into this awareness, it became very important for me to have patience with myself in order to keep moving in the right direction. It was critical to keep my eyes and ears open along with all other senses which seemed more heightened now. This worked for me in sports, professionally and through the years of caregiving. As the years went by taking care of Nancy, I realized caregiving was becoming the main purpose of my life. This process of setting goals yet not jumping too far ahead, has worked for me throughout life and particularly when Nancy became ill.

Phase Two is simply "what you think you want" years. This phase, if you live long enough, is about doing the distance. It is the longest phase. I say this because at the time, I was living day to day just looking for something. I was trying to figure out where I was headed. I was searching for the right answers to hopefully be on the right path. During this phase, many mistakes were made, choices I could not take back and challenges I needed to figure out. When we are young we do not necessarily think about the outcome, consequences, or where life will take us due to that choice. Set-backs are a part of this phase and how it is handled can affect life many years in the future.

The most important part of this phase is that I tried not to be physically or mentally harmed by my choices. Life will take different directions when we least expect it and adjustments will be needed, as changes happen. This will include disappointment at the price of having fun.

Phase Three is "learning to be mature years." This phase, at the time, was only half as long as phase two. This was the point when I realized I had to start to take life more seriously. The decisions I made were more critical in my development as a human being. Life, for me, at that time became uncertain with big changes. where I did my best to reach for the light. I continued to strive to make the right decisions, however, it was important for me to remember not all decisions are correct and they had ramifications. It was important to learn from my mistakes. This is how I came to understand just how critical it was to adapt to each situation as it presented itself. I also found it helpful to document my major decisions to alleviate potential mistakes in the future.

Phase Four is "knowing about maturity and the right thing to do for humanity." Springfield College had a logo which was "Spirit, Mind, and Body." I discovered, when I worked on my body with some form of physical activity, it strengthened my mind. It gave me the energy to focus on life decisions. Once focused, I then relied on my spirit to grow further.

Collectively, I felt I would be fortunate, entering this phase with an awareness of the world around me. Sometimes opportunities can be missed along the way while trying to find true purpose. In Earth's classroom, I continue to look for happiness for myself, but I will not complete my journey unless I contribute to humanity by being kind and generous with my time. Because of the work I am doing, I have the opportunity to peek over the mountain to get answers as to why I am here, perhaps, I already know. However, it will continue to take work and dedication. The beauty of it is, it's ultimately the greatest gift of all.

CHAPTER ONE

Phase One: Growing Up

I WAS RAISED BY TWO WONDERFUL PARENTS. MY MOTHER, Virginia was born and raised on Vineyard Haven, Martha's Vineyard, Massachusetts. Her mother, who was of Portuguese descent and her father, who was Cape Verdean, divorced after a short period of time. She was the youngest sibling. My grandmother raised my mother as a single mother after the divorce. Back in those days, people were not very respectful or accepting of mixed marriages. I was too young to understand the difficulty of a mixed relationship, but at that time, it wasn't approved. I can only imagine the strain it put on their relationship. My mother grew up with six other siblings, she had three sisters from a different father along with one sister and two brothers from a former relationship.

My mother graduated from high school on Martha's Vineyard. She was athletic, and played on the basketball team. Upon graduation, my mother decided to move to New Bedford, Massachusetts where her two sisters had two residencies. She went to secretarial school and pursued a career working in a legal office for several attorneys. After a few years, she met my dad, Guy. My dad, also of Cape Verdean descent, lived in New Bedford all his life. He was raised by a single mom near the Bay Village area. He enlisted in the Army in 1944 and was stationed in Bonn, Germany immediately at the end of World War II. When he returned to the United States he went back to school to receive his high school diploma from New Bedford Vocational. While working in a warehouse to help out his mother with the finances, he took a civil service exam and became a police officer in the city in 1951. My parents were married on January 31, 1954.

I was born November 20, 1954. We lived in a tenement on the third floor in the south end of the city on Thompson Street. Unfortunately, there was a fire on the second floor that Christmas so we had to move. Temporarily, we stayed with my mom's sister and husband, Esther and Arthur along with their boys, Nicky and Bobby. After that, we spent the next four years living at Blue Meadows Projects. It was a playground for kids like me, large families from very diverse backgrounds. At that time, my mom became pregnant with my sister so we needed more space. We moved to Weaver Street where I spent the rest of my childhood.

Back in those days, sadly and to this day, blacks and browns were not welcomed by everyone in the neighborhood. There was a petition to try to block my family from moving into that neighborhood. Fortunately, there were many neighbors who were appalled by that kind of action. We moved in, it was a wonderful neighborhood full of kids my age to play with. Everyone had a good-sized backyard. The largest yard we played in however, was the Rural Cemetery, which backed up to my house. There was plenty of space to learn how to play different sports. We would go out there every chance we could. Our neighborhood gatherings were consistent, we pushed each other with the occasional argument about the game, "is he in or out?" Friends in my neighborhood were very competitive. No-one was interested in losing, ever. I am grateful for a wonderful childhood where we created great friendships. My sister was born in 1959 so she benefited from the many kids who were around to play with too.

I attended the neighborhood school Congdon, which was within walking distance from my home. I made many friends at school. A few years later, when my sister started school, my mother began working in an attorney's office downtown. We had wonderful care from my great aunt Blanche and my great uncle Tony. I could not have asked for better people to take care of us when our parents were not around. My sister and I loved being with them whether it was on Weaver Street or at their home in Bay Village. We had the opportunity to make friends in both areas. It was quite the life!

I continued to learn different sports in the neighborhood and at school. At that time, I started playing organized baseball with the Greater New Bedford Little League. The team was the Verdean Vets mainly coached by Bucky Vincent and Kenny Barros. Even at that young age, around ten or eleven, I believe I recognized they were excellent human beings and very giving of their time to the community and its youth. After that, I began playing organized football with the New Bedford Boys Club coached by Bob Comeau who was married to my cousin Helen. My interest in sports continued and I became very engaged in watching professional sports on television, like the Boston Celtics, the New York Giants, the Boston Red Sox and the Boston Patriots.

I was in fourth grade when President John F. Kennedy was assassinated. Once again, I was too young to truly understand the impact or significance of this loss to our country. However, the memory of that day remains intact. On this day, my fourth-grade teacher, Miss Lopes, who was generally a gruff, no-smiles kind of person, stood in the front of the class with tears in her eyes and said, "our President has been shot and we are releasing you early." I knew that this was a great loss, but I didn't realize then, how great. It had to be big for Miss Lopes to show that emotion.

I went to Dunbar School in sixth grade. It was hard to leave friends. My teacher, Miss Friedberg, who happened to be the prettiest teacher at the time, moved me to the front of the class because she felt I needed glasses! Once I received glasses, my grades went up and my hitting average was much improved. It's amazing what you can do when you can see clearly!

I attended tenth grade at New Bedford High School (NBHS) in the fall of 1969. During sophomore year, there were riots in the West End of the city. My dad, being a minority police officer, was sent down to negotiate and to try to calm the situation. A couple of young people were killed in the city during the racial unrest. This was going on all over the country. Dr. Martin Luther King Jr. had been assassinated on April 4, 1968, as was Robert F. Kennedy, just after that on June 5, 1968. It was a crazy time in our American history. I was still young at the time, I didn't understand how the world worked outside of my small circle. It was the beginning of the fall and our city was under duress with riots in the West End. School was canceled and people were afraid. It was something I had never seen before. To learn we had a curfew was confusing. It took time for me to grasp the enormity of those events, but slowly I started to grasp the hatred and ignorance in the world. After the assassination of Dr. King, and the riots that followed around the country and in my own city, I eventually understood the inequality in our country and the true extent of the racism which was alive and well, then and today. It is shameful. My dad was involved with being a mediator with the rioters because the chief felt they could actually get something done having him involved. Within ten days, the city came back to normal and I was back in school.

During my three years at NBHS I was lucky enough to play sports. I always loved baseball so my sophomore year I tried out and played center field. Football was also a love of mine so I tried out my junior year. I made the team as a cornerback and earned the starting position after three interceptions. I was coached by Joe Bettencourt and his staff. Coach Bettencourt was all about toughness and pushed us beyond our limits, meaning, I always went further than I thought I could. Coach John Dell Isola was a wise and compassionate man whose wisdom was beyond words. I was grateful for that wisdom and his experience. He played in the early years of the NFL for the New York Giants. He also coached alongside Vince Lombardi for the New York Titans (AFL). They both taught me football was a game as close to representing life as any other example. It came with wins, losses, surprises, hard work, excitement, joy, disappointment and it could be humbling. This experience proved to be helpful to me later in life as I navigated the ups and downs that everyone faces.

When playing for the NBHS football team during junior year, our stamina was tested every day. We had to be in better shape than any other team. Our team record that year was 6-3. We did win the Bristol County League. I played center field in the spring for the varsity baseball team with Coach John Pacheco as the Head Coach. I was lucky enough to make the All Bristol County Team that year.

My senior year was an important year for me. My grades were good enough to make the honor roll and I kept them up the entire year. I was co-captain of the football team in my senior year. I had the privilege to block for the best running back in the state, David Reynolds. I was happy with accomplishments on and off the field. My high school experience was exceptional. I made lifelong friends who are still in my circle to this day. I am grateful for all the coaches I had at NBHS. They influenced me tremendously.

During the winter, I was invited to visit Springfield College to meet with head coach Ted Dunn. He appeared to be a great, dignified human being. The school had good academics and their sports teams were competitive. I was immediately accepted so I planned to attend Springfield the following fall.

After graduation, my summer job was to study the football playbook before attending camp in late August. Another piece of great news was that my dad was promoted to lieutenant for the New Bedford Police Department. He worked very hard to get there due to the politics involved in getting promoted in those days. Great things were happening with the Oliveira family.

My parents provided me with a great upbringing which lent itself to a foundation which helped me grow and become aware of my surroundings. Looking back, I did not realize the significance of the Civil Rights movement or the unrest in the 1960's, 1970's, and still seen today. We lost four important leaders by the assassinations of John F Kennedy (November 22, 1963), Malcom X (February 21, 1965), Martin Luther King, Jr. (April 4, 1968), and Robert F. Kennedy (June 5, 1968). There was so much going on during that decade however, with the events on January 6, 2021 it is clear racism and suppression is alive and well. There is still much work to be done. That being said, my parents protected me from the harm that racism caused at the time. They were acutely aware of the big and small injustices that existed and went on every day.

CHAPTER TWO

Springfield College

IN AUGUST 1972, I WAS PREPARING TO MOVE FROM MY home on Weaver Street to start football camp. Everything was moving fast. My friends from the Blue Meadows Projects gave me a great send off by throwing a big BBQ. My parents planned a cookout for the day before I was leaving. My Aunt Blanche, Uncle Tony, Gail, and friends Steve Gonsalves and Gary Brown were there for the sendoff. It was one final good-bye before leaving for college.

On the travel day to Springfield, I made sure I brought with me, other than clothes, the poster of my hero, Muhammad Ali. He became my hero because he sacrificed three and a half years of his prime boxing career to protest against the Vietnam War. He came back a different kind of fighter.

I remember the trip to the western part of Massachusetts. While driving up the Mass Pike I noticed the mountains in the distance. I grew up in the city, so this was new to me. There were thoughts and questions going through my mind. What will the next four years of my life be? My parents would not be there for me. Am I making the right decision?

We arrived at Springfield College where I met my former teammate Brian Rounseville in the parking lot. It was great to see a familiar face however, it was time to say good-bye to my parents. It was a sad good-bye, tears and all. After my parents left, Brian took me for a tour around the campus and re-introduced me to head coach Ted Dunn, as well as meeting some of the guys on the team. This was the first year freshmen could participate with the varsity squad. I was pleased to be invited. I was there to play fullback. Their offense was quite different from what I had ever played. They ran the triple option which is running offense with a lot of deception. Back in the 1970's, college teams used to run a new kind of offense where they would have three running backs in the back field with a quarterback. The fullback would be in front, which made it look like a triangle. The mission of the offense was to run the ball with many fakes and mis-directions to fool the other team on defense.

I majored in physical education which would certify me, upon graduation, to teach physical education, health and science. At the time, it did not mean much, adjusting to my new campus life was enough of a challenge. My residence was in a dorm called International Hall. This was quite fitting considering there were athletes from all over the country competing for a certain position in all sports. It was a real culture shock for me. It was the first time in my life that I was introduced to students with different nationalities from all over the world placed in a very small radius on a campus where we all lived together. It wasn't very long before I felt comfortable with campus life and the new routine of being on my own.

In week five, we had a bye-week which gave coaches a chance to make adjustments on defense. Unfortunately, my life took a painful turn. My uncle Tony passed away suddenly, I was devastated. It was the first time that I had lost someone so close to me. After returning to school from New Bedford after the funeral, I was offered to try out for the defensive end position. I learned how to play that position from a very smart coach, Frank Glazier. He had this cool, raspy voice and called me "Godfather." He thought I was Italian. I kind of enjoyed being called "Godfather." The movie had just come out.

By game five, I was given the opportunity to play and was pleased I was able to hold my own. I did everything I could to hold on to that starting position. I was happy to see my parents there. They were thrilled.

That evening I attended a concert on campus featuring the J. Giles Band. It was 1972. The warm up band was called Earth, Wind and Fire. I had no idea who they were at the time. I was thinking "are you kidding me?" They were unbelievable, and of course, we all know how it went for them. It was an amazing night to remember.

I continued to start the remainder of the season and in the end, our team was 0-9. A real bonus was that I had the pleasure of meeting some great brothers. The Battle twins, Stan and Stu, Macon Tucker from Georgia, Bill Grey from California, Ken Mitchell from Connecticut, and of course my roommate Mark Powers. I was enjoying life on campus and being introduced to the girls didn't hurt.

The second trimester started in winter after Thanksgiving break. It was the first time I was to be in Springfield during the winter. Chicago is famous for the Hawk and being cold, but Springfield had a challenging cold winter too. Mark and I shared a dorm room on the first floor. My bed was facing the north side of the parking lot. There were many nights I had to sleep in my arctic coat and getting motivated in the morning to go to class was a challenge.

I managed to pass all my classes and continued to enjoy campus life. At that time, "Sanford and Son" was on television with Redd Fox on Friday nights. I would go up to the third floor to watch it with Brian and Sam. This is where the nicknames Backstabbers and Malcolm were born.

In the spring trimester, I chose to try out for the Springfield College freshmen baseball team. My position was right field. It was nice to switch sports for a while. Before I knew it, the year played out quickly and it was time to go home. I continued to train for football along with working at the New Bedford Housing Authority. It was my old stomping ground at Blue Meadows Projects so I felt right at home. Sadly, in the middle of the summer our dog, "Boy" died. He was a part of our family, losing him was a loss that hit me hard.

I continued to play summer baseball for the American Legion not knowing it would be my last year of playing organized hardball. The summer flew by, and the next thing I knew I was back at camp in mid August. Brian and I traveled back with the hope of starting together at defensive end. Our names would become known as "old friends, bookends" (aka) "Backstabbers" and my name was now "Malcolm." We began with triple sessions and played on what was called Poly Turf. It was like playing on carpet. We endured many rug burns on our elbows and we were playing in high heat, as much as 120 degrees. It was exhausting. Brian and I put extra pressure on ourselves to make sure we would start together. We had a new defensive end coach whose name was Charley Casserly. He was a graduate assistant who had much knowledge of the position. He was also lead scout during game day. He would go to the game to learn what that particular team was doing the week before we were to play them. We had a great rapport with Charley. We knew we would be well prepared for our opponents that coming Saturday. We were tested on our strength, speed, agility and knowledge of our positions.

One afternoon between practice sessions, I decided to tie up a loose tailpipe on my parents' car. It had loosened while driving to Springfield earlier that week. I jacked up the car and got underneath, when I heard the sound of a car horn. I slid out to see that it was Stu Battle, who had graduated the year before. Just as we began to greet each other, the car dropped off the jack and crashed to the ground. I narrowly escaped being crushed. I knew at that moment that there was a guardian angel watching over me. The ramifications of what could have been hit me strongly, though I never spoke of it, instead, filing it away in the back of my mind.

That year Brian and I both earned the starting position at defensive end. We took great pride in that. "Old friends and Bookends" were indeed born. My roommate Mark and I moved to the third floor in our dorm. Brian lived on the same floor, needless to say, the third floor became party central.

I was enjoying campus life playing ball, focusing on classes, my new friends and parties. It was a good time in my life. Unfortunately, I injured my ankle playing against Northeastern University. I was out for two weeks. The one week that I couldn't practice I scouted with Charley and a few others to observe University of Rhode Island (URI) and to scout University of New Hampshire (UNH). They were having a great year. Charley asked me to time how long individual punts were in the air. It was a great lesson to understand what needed to be done to scout another team. I learned a great deal.

The following week, we practiced, but unfortunately, my ankle was still sore and weak. I was not able to play. Our team beat UNH 51-0. Brian had a great game. It had to have been the biggest upset in the country that day. We had one more game to go so I took great efforts to be ready to play in the next game with University of Bridgeport. They had won around 40 games in a row. We had to change what we were doing to meet their punter, Wayne Hamlet, who I was familiar with as he was a great player at Dartmouth High School, which neighbored New Bedford. We were at the end of the season and Charley invited us all downtown to his apartment for a break up pizza party to celebrate our year together.

I want to include a brief history about Charley. When he completed his graduate classes, he went to Washington D.C. to meet, at the time, head coach George Allen. As a result, he became a scout for the Washington Redskins. He moved up the ranks and ultimately became the General Manager of the team. They won at least one Super Bowl under his guidance before he became the first General Manager of the Houston Texans. Today, he can be seen on ESPN as an analyst. Charley explains the talents of the top prospects and teams in the NFL. You go Charley!

At the end of that year, Brian and I packed up and headed back to New Bedford. I needed a job and that summer I became a longshoreman. They paid very well and the heavy lifting was just what I needed to stay in shape. The City of New Bedford is historically well noted for being one of the richest fishing ports in the country. Longshoremen work in gangs of ten or more men who are hired to unload cargo from very large ships. My job was to unload frozen fish. Each box weighed close to a 100 pounds which were lifted by crane off the ship. Each ship usually took about three days. It was brutal work and very cold, so cold you had to wear winter gear to survive. As challenging as it was, the money was good and I stayed in shape.

Old friends, bookends arrived at football camp in late August of my junior year. At the start of camp, we knew we had a great chance of starting together. We had one last year as Brian was a senior. Luckily, we went through the season without any injuries, which is a win in itself. The season went by fast, ending with a record of four wins, six losses, but with great competition. We fought hard. I continued to live in the dorms on the third floor. College life was better than ever with extensive socialization and plenty of college friends and teammates. I was getting by with my classes, but it seemed like fun was the number one priority. The phrase, "having the time of your life" was never more true between sports and other extracurricular activities. I played one last year of varsity baseball and before I knew it, I was heading back to New Bedford for the summer.

In the summer after junior year, I delivered groceries for a local food market with my old friend Billy Olejarz. We had a good time and the bonus was a great workout. I also played on three different softball teams when I was not working. Then once again I found myself driving back to Springfield for my senior year and final football camp. I was acutely aware of how strange it felt to be without my other bookend. I understood life on campus would be different.

During my last pre-season practices, I was fortunate to have head coach Ted Dunn for my position coach, working with him one on one. It was his last season as head coach for Springfield College. I was determined to give it my all for this great man who coached over four decades. I was rewarded with the starting defensive end position for the fourth year in a row. That was an honor. I also became great friends with one of our offensive lineman, Dean McKissick, we are great friends to this day.

Two of my biggest games that season were against Southern Connecticut and the University of New Hampshire. Before the game I was asked to be the best man at my childhood friend's wedding. It was on a Friday night before the game the next day. Joe and Linda's wedding also gave me the opportunity to enjoy a quick visit with friends and family. My parents brought me back to Springfield early the next morning where I played my best game. It was an upset as UNH had been undefeated. It was so exciting. I remember my dad running on the field after the game. I was proud because he had such a glow in his eyes. There were tears falling down my cheeks. I still have a picture of my mom and me after the game.

My football career was over the following week. Upon reflection, my college playing days were over in a flash. An early lesson on how life passes you by quickly. It is a reminder of how important it is to seize the moment as it comes, because before you know it, it's gone.

That next winter trimester I was able to do my ten week student training in the neighboring town of Dartmouth, Massachusetts. It consisted of five weeks in the elementary school and five weeks at the high school teaching physical education. My friend Brian also did his student teaching at Dartmouth. We had much to talk about.

By the end of the trimester, finals were upon me and I barely got by. My parents came up for graduation. I remember their expression and how proud they were. It was a great moment in my life. After graduation my parents returned to New Bedford. I wanted to spend one more night with friends before heading home. The next day I drove around campus one more time as a graduate, I thought about how quickly four years went by and all the memories which would shape my life. It was a wonderful experience. As I drove home down the Mass Pike the question that came to me was "what comes next?"

During my college years, I began to clearly understand more about racism in this country and in the workforce. It affected my dad's journey in being promoted to higher levels in his profession. Ultimately, he did reach the level of Captain. He had to study five times more than the average person to score as close to the top of the list as possible. He was also faced with other favorites in line going for the same promotion. The key was to have a better score to guarantee a chance to make it. He became the first minority to achieve Sergeant, Lieutenant, and then finally Captain of the New Bedford Police Department. It is just another reason why he is still my hero.

My years at Springfield College were not just about academics and learning in the classroom but more importantly, interacting with students from all over the world and the country with different life experiences and backgrounds. This was enlightening for me as I came to know and understand everyone has a story to tell from their own life experience.

Playing football gave me the confidence to grow not only as a player and teammate, but as a person who understood what commitment to the task at hand really meant. I began to come out of my shell through these experiences and opportunities.

I was fortunate and with the presence of mind to understand the priceless tools gifted to me which would stay with me to this very day. I am grateful to the people I met along the way who taught me those lessons. Although I may never see them again, they made a positive and influential impact that will always be a part of me.

CHAPTER THREE

Phase Two: Exploring Adulthood

AGAIN, WHILE DRIVING HOME AFTER GRADUATION, MANY thoughts and questions ran through my mind such as: "What would life be like now that there is no school, no structure to the day? How will I earn a living?" I was certain I was not the only graduate thinking these thoughts. There was no reason for me to be any different. The reality in front of me at that time was that I was about to move back to my childhood home and my childhood room where things really had not changed. I had a vague thought that in the fall I would volunteer to coach football for the New Bedford Vocational High School.

That summer, I met the managers, Michael Sylvia and Mark Connors, of the Belmont Club, a local, popular nightclub. They offered me a position as doorman, which of course, I accepted. I worked at least five days a week. The owner, Bill Davidian, happened to be a great friend of my dad's. They had worked together on the police force for many years prior. It was wonderful to see him again. It was funny how things could boomerang back to you.

When fall arrived, I was looking forward to working with Clarence Brooks, who was a well-known and respected coach at New Bedford Vocational. Before the season actually got started, he was offered a position at his alma mater, the University of Massachusetts, Amherst. At that time I received a call from Head Coach Riley to take the offensive line coaching position. I immediately agreed, however, I thought to myself "I have no idea how to coach that position" and understood there was some learning ahead.

Before I started coaching, I was still working at the Belmont Club a few nights a week. That fall, I got reacquainted with my lifelong friend Lynn Donohue DiPetta, who is Bill's daughter. At the same time, I moved to Mattapoisett, Massachusetts with my friend Freddie. It was like being back in college. Apparently, I still could not get that lifestyle out of my system.

The summer raced along and I ended up enjoying my reconnection with old friends from New Bedford High School and playing softball with them. It was like an old, but new fraternity of the Whalers. We frequented the old regular haunts like Redwood Saloon and South of the Border. It was inevitable you would run into someone you knew.

Once I began coaching, it was a huge challenge. I didn't know much about the offensive line and needed a great deal of help along the way. I was fortunate to have Coach Riley and my great friend Kelvin Brooks, brother of Clarence Brooks (who had recently left to coach at UMASS) to help me out. He played offensive line for Boston University and had a deep knowledge of the position. Upon reflection, my head was not in the game, I was distracted and the effort needed to learn was simply not there, yet. Prior to this experience things came easy to me, no real effort was required. In hindsight, I blame myself. My priority was fun, not responsibility, I was not very mature for a twenty-one year old.

That winter, my dad attended the FBI Academy in Washington D.C. for several weeks. I would stop by with a watchful eye on my mom and grandmother (who had cancer) and my sister. In addition to looking after my family, I continued working at the Belmont Club and took an occasional school substituting job. That was my life at that moment. Eventually, my grandmother passed away that winter. It fell on me to make the decision to take her to the hospital. Her words haunt me to this day when they were wheeling her out of the house, she said "I am never going to come back here again, am I?" What does one say to someone who knows their end is near? My dad came back to check on her in the hospital, however, sadly, grandma only lasted a week. Experiences like these never leave you. At the age of twenty two, death still shocked and affected me deeply.

In the spring, I decided to take the Civil Service Exam to become a firefighter. I was thinking at the time that coaching and teaching was not going to work out for me. I also decided to move back home with my parents to reset and recharge. I came to the conclusion I was having way too much fun, making very little money, with no plans for the future.

When summer arrived, I continued to work at the Belmont Club enjoying the live music. There were two Jazz musicians who I became close to, Bobby Greene and John Harrison. Bobby was surely ahead of his time. He was a great saxophonist and equally, John on keyboard. Many gifted musicians have come out of the area and the New Bedford music scene is always happening. We were very lucky to have had the opportunity to hear them that summer. It was good fun for all.

At the end of the summer, I was hired to be the physical education teacher at the new Greater New Bedford Regional Vocational Technical High School, replacing the old vocational high school. I also passed the Civil Service Exam and was eligible to be a Firefighter. At the time, it did not seem like a big deal however, but I thank God I chose to follow the plan of becoming a teacher and coach. My goal when I attended college was to graduate to teach physical education somewhere. It made sense to me to have a job in the same field as my education degree. Having a teaching position offered me more avenues for available coaching positions. My degree was versatile, it gave me more opportunities to teach different subjects. I taught and coached that fall with my friend, John Quintal, who was a star athlete in his day at the same school. To this day, we remain friends.

In the fall of 1977 my teaching career began. My first challenge was to understand how the Physical Education Department worked and adjust along the way. It is not like taking a class when you were a student. When you become a teacher it is up to you to understand the dynamics of the classroom as a whole and the students individually and how they learn. It was my task to learn what worked and what didn't. It was a busy fall due to juggling three activities, it was not easy. I recognized that I was in my twenties and it was time to either sink or swim and accept the responsibilities that came with changes and growth.

I was given the opportunity to teach a health class to all the freshmen. Prior to this, I was not giving 100% into my career. More effort was needed if I was going to succeed. Apparently, my supervisor Jeff Riley saw something promising in me.

The notorious Blizzard of 1978 came that winter and as history recorded the whole region shut down for an entire week. It was something that had never been seen before. After the blizzard, I gained more confidence, I became much more social with my students, understanding their backgrounds and the strong influences that they faced in school and in the community. I did this by recognizing it was not just a job, it was a commitment to understanding the student needs. I continued to teach physical education and health and was rehired the following year. My commitment to education was not complete, it was clear to me my priorities needed to change if I wanted to be a professional teacher who motivated students. That year I developed a great friendship with Tom Gomes. He was back teaching at his alma mater where he started in basketball at the old Vocational High School. Tommy was, in my opinion, the greatest to come out of this area. I also connected with Lenny Sylvia during this time. We're friends to this day.

As spring moved into summer, I continued to work at the Belmont Club and play moderate pitch soft ball for a new friend Bonsie Silva. He bartended at the local bar, Genes' Cafe. He formed a great team and it was a lot of fun. On the side, I was still living like I was in college but my parents never stopped or lectured me. However, as I would head out the door, my dad would say "use your head" with his familiar "look."

During my second year of teaching, I was aware of how much I needed to focus on my career. At this time, my life-long friend Mike Shea joined the physical education department staff as well as part of the coaching team for the varsity football team. By winter, the Belmont Club scene had run its course and live entertainment ended. That gave me the chance to put more effort into my teaching career, although my social activities were still in full swing. In November of that year, I met Sheryl Brulotte who became my partner and ultimately my wife with the relationship lasting for ten years. I was too immature at the time to understand what love was. We had great times together for sure, but the marriage didn't last. Those memories still bring a smile. The Brulotte family was always wonderful to me and my family.

CHAPTER FOUR

Career and Relationship

WHEN WINTER ARRIVED, MY SISTER GAIL ACCEPTED A dietitian position at a hospital in the Daytona Beach, Florida area. My dad and I drove her to Florida with all her belongings. It seemed just like yesterday when we were all living on Weaver Street with no responsibility. We had quite an adventure. On our way through Philadelphia, we heard Teddy Pendergrass was in a terrible car accident. He survived, but sadly, he was wheelchair bound for the rest of his life. I used to listen to him when he was with The Blue Notes. I still do.

That summer, a position opened up with the Massachusetts Migrant Program. It was a program highlighted specifically for migrant students in the city for extra schooling and different activities and events. I worked for this program for many years as a physical education teacher located at the new Voc-Tech school.

At the same time, my mother, who owned property on Martha's Vineyard, had been paying property taxes on a piece of land. My grandfather had divided the land up for each sibling to have a place on the Vineyard. My parents built a one bedroom cottage on a beautiful spot. It was our future summer place that now holds many great memories.

During my third year of teaching, I discovered that coaching football was becoming more enjoyable, not just a job. I learned about the different positions and schemes which teams ran to outnumber their opponents. Even though I never knew how to play chess, I understood the premise of it. The game of football was like a chess game for me. It was fun to see what I could do to make things easier for the players. We usually played our freshmen games on Friday nights. On Saturday John Q, Lenny and myself would scout the opposing team for the next week. It was becoming clear that teaching and coaching was actually my destiny.

It was getting to the point where I was looking for a more stable life. Dating and clubbing seemed like too much work. I continued to spend my free time working out and with my friends and having fun was still on my menu. I even had the opportunity to dabble in a little officiating for winter track meets. I was the "starter" for all running events. I imagine you that you are all familiar with "on your mark, get set, GO." I was also involved with coaching girls' softball for a few years at Vocational Tech. This was a new program that we had just started. It was not a bad way for me to make some extra cash and it was enjoyable working with the student athletes .

I was offered a coaching job with the varsity team with head coach Mike Shea. Our staff was made up of friends including Lenny, Fred G and Johnny Q. My coaching positions included offensive backs and defensive ends. I felt things were coming together.

The next year, football season was a sub-par year, however we knew there would be a better team the next year. These players had future goals. They worked out during the off season and they were dedicated to a consistent conditioning schedule. In the meantime, I continued to officiate track. Occasionally, I would get a surprise visit from Clarence who continued to coach the defensive line, now, at Syracuse University. My rule was to be available to Clarence anytime. When he was in town, we would always meet up and go out for the evening.

Our football program was on the rise and we felt comfortable with our system. Mike Shea made me offensive coordinator. I truly enjoyed playing that chess game of figuring out what the opponent was doing and how to break down plays to have the best advantage. Coaching was becoming an important part of my life.

During the spring of 1987 I traveled to Florida to pick up my new English Bulldog puppy who I named Jocko. He was very beautiful. He had a gentle temperament and was a joy to be with. Shockingly, within eleven months he suddenly passed away. Apparently, his trachea closed which stopped his breathing when we were at the veterinarian's office. It was shocking to all of us. Then, at the same time, my Uncle Arthur passed away suddenly. These tremendous losses began to change me. Reality was setting in as well as depression. These deaths affected me deeply and left a lingering sadness that I couldn't always ignore. The fantasy life I had been living was disappearing as the realities of life presented themselves. I began to reflect upon everything and asked myself "Is this the way I wanted to live the rest of my life?" I didn't know at the time what it was, what I did know however, was that something had to change.

During that time, I received a call from the head coach at New Bedford High School who wanted to offer me a coaching position. I actually declined twice because I was fearful of more change, but the third time I accepted.

I took a bike ride to see a girls' softball team who qualified for the State playoffs. My friend Ken Soares was the coach along with Wayne Hamlet. If you recall, he was the punter at Bridgeport when we were in college. Coach Wirth was in the field house. I was surrounded by them, including my old coach, Dan Conceicio. I wanted the opportunity to coach at NBHS, but athletic coaches needed to work in the same school system. The agreement came with an offer for a job at an elementary school named Pulaski along with the coaching position. The decision was difficult as I was leaving many friends and stepping into unknown territory. I was appreciative for the years at New Bedford Voc-Tech. I learned a great deal which I knew would lend itself well to my new experience in another school system and football program.

In summary, I am grateful for those ten years of fun memories, new situations, and encounters with new people that shaped my adult life. Those experiences helped me become a better teacher and coach. I settled into the new routine and school environment. I became comfortable in my new home. The loss of Jocko and my Uncle Arthur was a serious blow. The pain of losing loved ones was a pain I was beginning to get used to. They all affected me deeply and I always felt like I lost something in my heart. I miss Jocko to this day.

CHAPTER FIVE

Michael meets Nancy

IN THE FALL OF 1988, I BEGAN A NEW JOURNEY. I HAD been coaching at my alma mater and teaching physical education at Pulaski Elementary School. It was a whole other world for me as I was used to teaching high school students who were between the ages of fourteen to eighteen. The transition to teaching students who were between the ages of five to eleven took some getting used to. It was a very different mindset and I understood I was back in another learning stage of my professional development.

On the first day I met our principal, Larry Gibbs. I could tell we were going to get along. He appeared to be a caring man who had the skill and talent to keep the troops together. I knew I would learn from him. I understood I needed to give students a sense of having fun and releasing energy during the time we had together. I was also faced with coaching a defensive line with a new staff. It took time to master this new system of coaching and teaching, but I was eager to learn.

After a while, the teaching became familiar and coaching with Joe Wirth and the staff was the beginning of a great experience. His coaching method and style were second to none. I learned the sophistication of how a game should be coached. Not only did I enjoy and learn a great deal my first year at NBHS, the team was very successful.

As the season ended and winter arrived, my schedule became a comfortable routine. I stayed at home mostly, however, I did manage to have some fun. I realized then too, my home was lonely without Jocko. His death affected me more than I had anticipated. Dog lovers would understand this. Dogs become a part of the family and we typically last longer than they do so we are impacted by the loss of another family member. That being said, another English Bulldog came into my life that spring. I named him Winston. He was the cutest puppy and great to come home to, however, there was still something missing. I felt the need to expand my circle more.

Toward the end of the school year, I began to notice a black Cadillac arriving in the mornings where I had outside duty escorting the students across the street. I enjoyed greeting the students and their parents. It gave me the opportunity to connect with both. The woman in the Cadillac was very attractive, dressed to the nines and clearly caught my eye. She would roll down her window and always came out with a sassy or funny statement towards me. She had a look of confidence and a smile I will always remember. We continued with pleasantries, but a meeting outside of school did not happen for a while. Through a short chat, I learned she was the school adjustment counselor. Her name was Nancy Hinkley. Her office was in the main lobby of the building away from my gym so we did not actually meet until spring. Watching her walk away I would say to myself, "who is that fine lady?" We finally connected outside of school to learn more about each other. At the time, she was in the middle of getting a divorce as I was. I found speaking with her to be very easy. I enjoyed her confidence, her laugh, her smile and her great sense of humor. She intrigued me. Every time we got together we enjoyed each other's company.

When summer arrived, I moved to a third floor apartment in New Bedford. Winston was now with my parents. He was in good company with their beautiful black shepherd J.D. Winston was really better being there. I was away from home a lot and had constant company at my place. Winston needed more attention than I could offer with my hectic schedule. At that time, I was feeling yet another change was on the way and welcomed it with open arms. I felt I had known Nancy all my life. She made it so easy. I found myself always looking forward to seeing her. The major bonus, by the way, was, she knew how to cook. We were together quite a bit that summer as I prepared for another football season. Again, I found myself unsure of my future, however for some reason I knew Nancy would be by my side. I will always remember her saying to me, "whatever you want, I want." I took that to mean to enjoy my life as I will be there with and for you. At that point, I counted on her for support and she followed through every time.

That fall, I continued to teach at the same elementary school and coached football, the difference now was that Nancy worked there too. She provided constant support and unconditional love, which made me very happy.

I discovered life was different, more exciting and full. The staff and making new friends had become easier and provided a sense of stability and contentment. I also realized I was becoming more and more committed to Nancy. Over time, we developed a beautiful formula for a successful relationship.

We spent the Christmas holiday respectfully with our own families that winter. For New Year's Eve, I met a few of Nancy's friends at Karen and Fernando Garcia's home. It turned out Karen and I both graduated the same year from New Bedford High School. It is a small world.

My life was more exciting now as we enjoyed each other's company. Although we still lived in our respective homes, we were spending more and more time together. It was a joy to wake up to her cheerful smile as if to say, "it's going to be a great day, baby, because you have my total support." How could I possibly go wrong? Our routine included working out four days a week. I would stay at her place and she at mine, it was working for both of us.

One night, I got a call from my old friend, Clarence, who was still coaching at Syracuse University. He happened to be in town so he came by the apartment to see me. Spontaneously, Nancy came out of the spare room. The look on Clarence's face was hilarious. He looked at me, then at her, then back to me and said, "what the?" Both Nancy and I said "Surprise!" After that, Nancy and Clarence would always be clowning around. It was the greatest feeling to know my friend enjoyed the company of my girl and she did his. During one of his visits, Clarence shared that he had been offered the job of defensive line coach for the Chicago Bears. Dave Wannstadt, who had worked with Clarence in the past at NFL camps, was now the head coach and brought Clarence on board. Of course, he accepted the position and we painted the town red in celebration of his new position. I think I was more excited than he was. So, naturally I instantly became a Chicago Bears fan. It was a real thrill to receive his Saturday night calls before the game and then Sunday after the game. It was great fun cheering him on. Who knew that one of my best friends would be coaching in the NFL?

DON'T TAKE IT FOR GRANTED

In the spring, Nancy and I took a trip to the Bahamas. It was the first time we traveled together and it turned out to be wonderful. My travel itinerary was limited to being on a bus with athletes and coaches going to games which was an experience in and of itself. Traveling for pleasure wasn't something I had spent much doing up to this point. Being with Nancy made it easy. It was apparent that we would have more pleasurable travel experiences in the future.

That summer, I moved again, to the home of my Aunt Elsie and Uncle Harry. They had passed away so the house was available. My dad was instrumental in this move. It was a great location, with off street parking, closer to school, the field and Nancy's house. It was a good year as our relationship was thriving.

I began to socialize again with my cousins Bobby and David on Saturday afternoons and Nancy would join us. Bobby and I grew up together with his brother David and as kids, we would play games. As we got older, we would get together after he finished work on Saturday to enjoy a few libations and laughs. As Christmas approached, I thought that it was time to introduce Nancy to my parents as the "love of my life." I would call it "Livin La Vida Loca" and for years, life seemed to be on a positive course, happy, with good friends, great family and Nancy brought more joy. I had hit the lottery!

On championship Sundays with the NFL, I began a new tradition. I would invite friends over for food and drink when the top four teams play to see who would go to the Super Bowl. Nancy would go shopping with her friends while the men acted like boys. It was a beautiful thing!

During the spring break Nancy and I traveled to St. Pete's Beach in Florida. It was a great trip; so much so we didn't want to come back. We promised we would return in the future, which we did many times over the years.

At the end of the year 1991, due to budget cuts, my job was at an end. I spent most of the summer wondering what direction my future was taking. Even so, Nancy and I spent our time going to the beach, the cottage on Martha's Vineyard, but reality was heavy on my mind. Job insecurity is something teachers live with, but I was anxious to discover what would happen next in my career.

Not wanting to waste time, I spoke with the school district superintendent, Mr. Nanopoulos, to see if there were any positions available. During our conversation, Mr. Nanopoulos saw that I was certified in science (however, I had never taught it). As it so happened a science teacher at Normandin Junior High School had recently retired, the position was open. The timing was perfect. He offered me the position, which I took knowing full well I had my work cut out for me. It would be another learning curve teaching eighth grade science and coaching football. The good thing, I was up to the challenge. I was fortunate, being new to the school, to have a very helpful teaching staff to assist me in learning the ropes of traveling from room to room teaching a subject I had to first learn about. It was indeed a challenge, however, it was a whole lot easier having support from people who became friends along the way.

The fall of 1991 ended up being Coach Joe Wirth's last year which was a tremendous loss for me. He chose to coach football at University of New Haven. Coach Wirth has impacted how my life developed to this day. Had I not known Coach Wirth I would not have met Nancy.

We finished out the year taking road trips with friends to Patriots games in Bill Gathright's van. Life in general carried on and was great. Nancy and I took our second trip to St. Pete's Beach in the spring, then New York City to see my first Broadway Show "Miss Saigon" which was unbelievable. Nancy was opening my eyes to so many new experiences.

The following year (1992) I transferred to yet another school to work at Keith Junior High School teaching seventh grade science. It was closer to home as well as the football field and I felt it was a good move for me even though I missed my friends at Normandin.

The fall football season was different in many ways. Wayne Hamlet, the punter from Bridgeport moved up to head coach, all the other coaching positions remained the same. I was about to be teaching seventh grade Life Science which was focused on how different living things on Earth function and develop. The key was how I planned to engage with thirteen and fourteen year old students. Again, a new learning curve was in store for me. I decided to start simply by giving students a task. I called it the science Bible. Each student was responsible for bringing their science notebook to class each day. If they entered class without it, they weren't allowed to retrieve it. Most work was done in their notebook. The message was if you brought your notebook to class each day you could not fail my class. I wanted them to take the responsibility seriously so they would succeed. I was not there to teach them only science, I was there to teach them how to successfully study and learn also. My lesson plans varied from Level 1 to Level 4 which was average to advanced. I enjoyed the concept and the students responded well.

Meanwhile, coaching was a challenge. We had many talented players, however, they were all learning their positions. It was an average season, but I was optimistic and felt the future was bright. It was that year I developed "the walk". Before each game, I took all starters to the field to speak about the upcoming game. It was my intention to give a little more spice to inspire the players to over-exceed their playing ability. I am not going to embellish on my special tactics as it might incriminate me. It apparently worked.

DON'T TAKE IT FOR GRANTED

Nancy and I took our first cruise to Puerto Rico for a week that winter with friends, which was wonderful. We went with a group of teachers who we worked with, so it was nice being with each other in a party environment. I found myself relaxing, talking with colleagues and getting to know their stories. Life was looking good from all angles. I planned on staying here for a while. Later that year Nancy and I took our third trip to St. Pete's Beach. Nancy was a wonderful travel companion. I got great pleasure from it.

The following year of 1993 was a very special year. The football team had many talented players from the city. They had to prove they were the real deal, expectations were high. It did not take long to see that this New Bedford team had a chip on their shoulders. They took it out on every opponent and it was apparent they were on a mission. One Friday night, we had an away game against a highly competitive team. One very serious message came out of that game. It was clear, racism reared its ugly head. Players on the opposing team were very aggressive with their taunting and I genuinely felt for our players. Sadly, we lost the game and had to suck it up and hope for a re-match.

I believed, at that time, our players were ready to finish the rest of the season without a loss. Well, we qualified for the Super Bowl in Division 1 in Massachusetts and we got our wish. A rematch with the same team. Our team got their sweet revenge by beating them to win our first Super Bowl 45-10. I have to say that was the greatest football victory of all in my life and I will cherish it always as will our players. It was outstanding to witness that in the end, racism lost. It was a great year for coaching.

I was experiencing a terrific year, I was comfortable and satisfied with my teaching position, grateful for family and friends and being with my beautiful Nancy. I even got the chance to visit with my dear friend Charley Casserly when Washington came to play the New England Patriots. I met with Charley and he shared with us his story about how his journey evolved. It could not get any better than that.

During that summer Nancy and I were doing our normal workouts, beaching and spending time on the Vineyard where I focused on the following fall football season. I was looking forward to working with some of the most talented players ever at New Bedford High School. Forgive me Alumni, but they were probably the most talented group of players I ever coached. I smile to myself as I write this.

CHAPTER SIX

The Big Move

IN THE FALL OF 1994 WE WON THE SUPER BOWL. OUR football team dominated every phase of the game and became the first undefeated/untied team in recent history. They won their second Super Bowl title and were ranked twenty-fifth in the country. It was a glorious season to be part of and we were all thrilled. In addition to this, New Bedford High School won titles in track, basketball, volleyball and baseball. It was an exceptional year, and one for the books!

I even had the chance to meet Hank Aaron, the Hall of Fame baseball player to hit over 740 career home runs and known as the 'home run king' based on Biographer Terence Moore as of October 5, 2022. More than Babe Ruth. This chance came about because the father of one of our players, Joe Andrews, knew Hank Aaron from the minor leagues. We had a perfect day and spent most of that day together before the fundraiser which he flew in for that night. I had the pleasure of driving the limousine to T.F. Green Airport in Providence with Joe Andrews, Wayne Hamlet, the Gridiron Club President, Manny Bettencourt, and a state trooper. A special picture was taken of me with Nancy, my mom and dad. It is a priceless memory.

That spring, Nancy and I took our annual trip to St. Pete's Beach. We always enjoyed our time there, unfortunately, this time, the news from home was not good. Nancy's father, Tony, experienced a heart attack and was in a Boston hospital. When we returned, he had been transferred to a rehab in New Bedford. Later in the spring on Memorial Day weekend he passed away. His passing deeply affected Nancy as she was daddy's little girl and in turn this affected me deeply, for her. I was there to support her as I understood a part of her had been taken away. We created a very strong bond which helped with working through the grief. I believe that was the first real test Nancy and I had to endure during our relationship to this point.

Our football team performed beyond our expectations in the fall of 1995. They won 8-2 and qualified again for the Super Bowl for the third straight year. Unfortunately, they lost in the close. It was a low scoring game, however, the kids had a great season and were all pleased with that.

At the time, my science classes were doing well. I added more to the lesson plans so the kids were busy with work and fun. I was pleased my organizational skills were improving which I believe showed the students consistency and commitment to them as their teacher. Life at home continued as we enjoyed spending our time with friends and family as well as special Friday nights with drinks, delicious food, and dancing. I can feel myself smiling right now. I was definitely with the only person I wanted to be with for all time.

That fall, my Aunt Blanche's health was declining. If you recall, in an earlier chapter, she and my uncle Tony took care of me and my sister when my parents worked. It was a very difficult time to witness yet another person so close to me, to us, going through the sad, end days of life. She passed early in the fall and the only feeling I was experiencing was numbness.

I began the new school year on a sad note; however, I knew the show must go on, right? Our football team did not make it to the Super Bowl that season however, my students were a constant joy to work with. The other joy to enter our lives was an adopted West Island Terrier. Nancy's mom was unable to take care of her any longer. Her name was Tasha. It became apparent our independent lives were going to need some adjustments. I nicknamed her "wise ass" probably for obvious reasons. We were grateful for Nancy's mom to take care of Tasha during our annual visits to St. Pete's Beach where we discussed adopting another dog so Tasha would have some company. We installed a pet door down stairs in the basement to allow the dogs to come and go freely into the back yard which was enclosed. We took a trip to Milford to check out golden retrievers. We fell in love with a black lab mix, two years old and gentle as can be. We named him Slate.

It was the fall of 1997, and again, here we were qualifying for the Super Bowl. We just couldn't bring it home. My classes however and teaching in general seemed to get better. I was committed to making a difference each year. That commitment rewarded me with being inducted into the New Bedford High School Gridiron Hall of Fame. It was a real honor. The Whalers always had a great tradition of winning. Many great players were participants in the program. The best part of the honor came with being nominated by my former high school coach, Joe Bettencourt. My parents and

Nancy were in attendance and many of my friends that supported the Gridiron Club, who raised money for our football program. It was a great night and it was clear my parents and Nancy were very proud.

We decided to change things up in the spring and went to Aruba. Aruba was a great change for us. We had never traveled that far from home. We spent hours in the spectacular blue water, everything was close by and the service was impeccable.

I also managed to pull off a surprise 50th birthday party for Nancy. I surprised her by having her think we were simply going out. About 150 people showed up. We had a great night. Nancy was surprised that I could pull it off. She never showed that look of surprise, it was more a look of appreciation.

The summer months were spent the traditional way that we had established over these years going to the Vineyard and Onset beach. During this particular summer we enjoyed an added bonus from my sister Gail. She was in the process of moving back here from being away for the better part of twenty years. She had been looking for a house in New Bedford. Guess who was there to help her? Well, it was Nancy. She found Gail a beautiful home in the North End in a great neighborhood. It was a wonderful thing to have the Oliveira family back in the same city. Having Gail return home made us now feel full again. Gail worked as a dietitian and had moved around quite a bit from Florida, Virginia, Long Island, New York and now she was in New England. She had quite the resume. Nancy and Gail got on like sisters so it was easy when we got together with her boyfriend Derek who happened to be from

England. This offered an international flavor to the mix. Derek was very funny and he loved our family gatherings. Of course, he loved soccer, where I love the American game of football. That never got in the way.

My science classroom improved again as I added more skills which included exercises to improve student learning while keeping their interest. On Friday, if the class was well behaved during the week, the students would be able to participate in scientific games. They would practically run the class with scientific questions from the entire year. I came up with a chart, a chart which was based on behavior and would reflect that. Based on getting an A = 10.0 being excellent down to 6 being poor, 8 being good would afford them their Friday classes of fun. My lesson plan allowed every student a chance for success. If you recall, in an earlier chapter, students were required to bring their science notebooks to class each day where the entire year of work was summarized and organized. They understood they would not fail my class if they brought the book. It would be impossible because I would check their books and quiz them on the material every day.

Our holidays were joyful now that Gail was part of our celebrations. Right on time, that year we received bad news about my favorite cousin Nicky. He passed away suddenly. He was putting up a Christmas tree and collapsed from a heart attack. We were heart broken and it naturally took all the joy out of our holiday. My memory of him was of an older brother who always included us in all of his ongoing activities. He always played Top 40 music in his band, as well as teaching music on Cape Cod. He was pretty cool and is still dearly missed and will always be remembered.

The rest of the year mimicked the years before, spending time in our favorite get-a-way spots. We enjoyed the pattern of our lives. We were not up for any surprises. You know the saying no news is good news. We did receive good news however, when we learned my dad was invited by the Mayor of New Bedford to serve as Chairman to the City's Licensing Board. He accepted and as a family we were proud of his achievement. It was a compliment and a reflection on his continued commitment to his community and the city of New Bedford.

The fall of 2000 was a bittersweet one. Our football team did not perform well. It was a challenge to motivate this group. The differences in the talent in the football team this year were a combination of experience and talent. Each team we met was either rebuilding their system or at the peak of their performance.

On the other hand, once again, my classes were very motivated and we had fun. In the classroom, it is a mixture of the upbringing of each student and what a teacher needs to do to engage them. Too much free time will create boredom and possible discipline problems. The challenge was creating a stimulating, exciting learning environment. Each day was a pleasure to teach these kids. Going to school every day with a smile on my face was a real pleasure and a gift. When I look back, I have to say it was the peak of a great life experience because the things I could control were predictable and getting better especially in my profession. My home life was excellent.

As much as I disliked change, it was time to move in another direction. That spring I put my name in for the school's Attendance Officer position, which is also known as a Truant Officer. The main role was to keep track of student attendance and behavior. I worked with many "at risk" families. I wanted to make a difference in their lives. The first challenge was, I was required to leave my current students ten weeks prior to the end of the year. I was deeply saddened by this as they were. I had to believe all was good in the end as we all learn from change.

Those ten weeks introduced me to how the Juvenile Court worked which I found interesting and enjoyed meeting my fellow attendance officers around the district. It was quite a contrast from being in the classroom. I learned about probation, the department of social services and working with the attorneys; it was very exciting. Those ten weeks prepared me for the workload of the next year. Through this job I was able to work with our Superintendent, Mike Longo. I discovered him to be a great man, leader and friend. It was comforting to know everyone had each other's back.

The Twin Towers were attacked on September 11, 2001. It was very strange not knowing what really happened. It took time for us to learn what was actually going on. The announcement came over the PA and all the afternoon activities were canceled. It was surreal going home and witnessing the tremendous horror on television and seeing what happened to the twin towers in New York City. It didn't become real until we understood the amount of lives lost at what we now call Ground Zero. I recall returning to work the next day feeling different with the knowledge our world in the United States was changed forever. We don't realize how precious life is and how we take it for granted.

This epic event was the beginning of my year as an Attendance Officer. I was responsible for overseeing eight elementary schools and also Keith Junior High School. The job involved more responsibility during after school hours, so I had to make a decision about coaching. The decision was difficult, however, in order for me to do my job right, I needed to make that difficult choice. It would be my final year of coaching high school football. The memories of coaching those fine young men over the years at Voc-Tech and Bedford High School were priceless. I still run into former players and feel I would not have done anything differently. Leaving was bittersweet.

At that point I was free to concentrate on my new job. I was spending more time at the Juvenile Court working with other probation officers, social services and attorneys. It was a very different world; however, I loved it. At the time, our sitting judge was Bettina Borders. I believe we had a great working relationship from the start. Everyone was fair. Everyone treated me as I did them, with respect.

Judge Borders started a Drug Court at Juvenile Court where I represented the School Department. Every Tuesday, our team would report to the judge the statistics from each student involved. We would check the students who were taking drugs and give them the opportunity to get clean. It was a different spin on the job however, I enjoyed it and wished to be involved.

That spring Nancy decided to change her job from School Adjustment Counselor to being involved in a new program targeting young students with learning issues. Her talents and abilities lent themselves well to being more involved in the entire school system versus one school. During the summer months we had plenty of time to prepare for the next year. I was happy for Nancy and felt she deserved this change.

As it happened the next year, my old little league coach, Dan Conceicio asked me if I could help out with his team, naturally I accepted. The practices were at night and it fit into my schedule. He wanted me to run the offense, so that was different but I understood how it worked due to the experience I had and I looked forward to motivating young players again on the playing field. It was great to work with Danny again and he encouraged me to call all the plays. The season was a long one because it started the first week of August and ended in November. I enjoyed working with younger boys teaching them the football system, it was rewarding as the boys were learning skills they would use as they moved forward to high school. The bonus was that the team made the playoffs.

Being an Attendance Officer was a change from being a teacher. I got a real sense of what our city youth needed. Working with at risk families was another learning curve. I realized many of our failing students had minimal to no support at home, which created more problems for them not only in school but also out on the streets. School was the last thing on their minds in order to survive. The opportunity to visit student homes gave us the answer to why the child was not performing well in school. For some, the living conditions were horrible and understanding that, the courts had to get involved and more professional help was needed.

We learned in the spring our friend Bill Gathright, who was the head of sporting communications at UMASS Dartmouth had a circulation problem in his leg which ultimately led to the amputation of his leg. This was shocking and very tough on all of us. He was a good friend. I visited him in rehab often. His spirits were high, which helped. Bill adjusted well after rehab and ended up going back to work. We were all very happy for him.

The following fall of 2003 was my first year not coaching football in 26 years. My full attention went to my new job and my responsibilities were growing. I had a full plate, which I welcomed.

That winter, the drug court was run by a federal grant and our team qualified to attend three conferences. The first was in San Antonio, Texas, it was a five day conference. During that time Nancy traveled with friends to Florida for a week while I was at my conference. It was the first time we spent that much time apart. It was a strange feeling, I had a heartache knowing I was going to miss her. I did enjoy the conference, it was informative and I had the opportunity to work with everyone on our team including Judge Borders. It was interesting to collaborate with the professionals we came to admire, and discovered they were actually normal human beings like everybody else outside of work. I got to see the humorous side. There were opportunities to meet professionals from all over the country. I neglected to mention the conference was held right by the RiverWalk in San Antonio. Everything was top shelf. We all had our own beautiful room with great food and service. It was awesome to relax with people from the conference which was conveniently close to the sights and entertainment. It will always be an experience to remember. I looked forward to the next conference which was held in Philadelphia. The networking was exciting and informative. We enjoyed having fun during the down times.

In the spring I was appointed to the court liaison position for the school department by Superintendent Michael Longo. My task was to figure out the best way to create a new position and make sure it worked for students, families, school and court systems. It was important for me to be sure to keep the lines of communication open between the Superintendent and the Judge. I was responsible for providing information to Probation, Social Workers and the Principal of any situation which involved an "at risk" student, a case at a time. I reported all my cases to Probation and the Judge. Most of my time was spent in Juvenile Court. This way, the attendance officers did not have to hang around the court waiting for their cases to be called and in general things ran much smoother. I enjoyed working closely with the court personnel and the judges especially, Judge Borders. I enjoyed my position and made sure I did my best to make it an important, relevant position. The other bonus was that I shared my office downtown at the old New Bedford High School building with Nancy, along with a number of other women who were friends of ours.

During this time our careers were on different committees but there was one that we both shared, The Diversity Committee of the New Bedford Public School system. Marlene Roderiques, our Assistant Superintendent of Diversity, headed up the committee. Nancy was responsible for getting out into the community, organizing ethnic foods from different restaurants in the city for our Gala celebration for diversity. The event was held at New Bedford High School. Everyone enjoyed the amazing food presented. Nancy was one of the recipients awarded for her hard work and success of the event which was held at City Hall. This is yet another reason I was so proud to be her man. She was a class act.

I will always remember the fall of 2004. It started with my third conference trip, which was in Chicago. Our Drug Court team went there at the beginning of September. We had great weather, it was a beautiful city and the people I met at all three conferences were there. These conferences taught us how to engage the youngsters who were experiencing issues which could potentially lead to early drug use. The bottom line was each drug court needed to speak their language, We brainstormed and shared ways of getting these at risk students the attention needed to help direct them down a more successful path. It was an exceptional education. In addition, I had the opportunity to enjoy the Navy Pier and the Chicago Cubs at Wrigley field.

That same year the Red Sox won their first world series in 86 years! It was the same year my dear friend Bill Gathright got rushed to a Boston hospital for heart surgery. He had a 30% chance of survival. The day before the surgery, my friends Ken Soares, Bob Simmons, and I went to see Bill. We gave him a taste of our humor to ease the pressure and distract him from the surgery, hoping it was helpful. Bill passed away the next day. The complications from poor circulation were more than the doctors could handle. We were all devastated. I could not believe he was gone. He was at all our memorable events and was like a brother to me. I miss him dearly, we all do. He was the biggest Cleveland Browns fan ever.

The holidays were celebrated that year as usual however, I felt an empty place in my heart for my boy Bill. It was still too fresh in my mind and soul. Life continues, but Bill was deeply missed when the fellas got together. For my fiftieth birthday Nancy bought me a Plasma TV, which became an amazing entertainment center. How could you not love this beautiful woman!? Naturally, I had the fellas over that championship Sunday because the Patriots were in it for the third Super Bowl out of four years. Of course, we watched it on my new Plasma TV! The Patriots won that Super Bowl. We could see the dynasty among us. It eased some of the pain of losing so many of our dear people.

During the summer of 2005 I threw Nancy a surprise retirement party. She was planning on working after retirement with the school department and the parents of preschool students. It was a fine party with family and friends, all enjoying eating and dancing. I was very proud to show Nancy all the appreciation for her thirty-five years in the school system and knowing she had so much more to give. She had helped so many struggling parents along the way. There was nothing that could match the value of her work ethic.

My job shifted again in the fall of 2005 when I became responsible for and required to be a member of different advisory committees. I joined the board of Brick by Brick. The founder was Lynn Donahue DiPetta at the time. Lynn was a friend from back in the days at the Belmont Club. She formed a club where at-risk students could put musical and artistic skills to the test. It was another place for students to be in an educational learning environment together, outside of school. I was also on the New Bedford High School advisory board and drug court. My days were full and very rewarding.

In the late spring at the Juvenile Court, there were different judges who would sit on the bench, just as Judge Borders was the sitting judge in New Bedford. I had the fortunate opportunity to meet Judge Mark Lawton, who introduced me to several former New England Patriots. They were hoping to put together a camp where former star players could work with the kids and area coaches. They were great guys and it was fun to put that week of instruction together. They worked mainly with the New Bedford High School head coach Dennis Golden and Dan Canceicio who was the New Bedford Bears head coach, and Pop Warner head coach. It was a successful camp. Our superintendent Mike Longo helped to finance the camp. It was amazing to connect the New England Patriots with the New Bedford community. I was proud to be a part of it.

Nancy and I took our usual summer trips to Martha's Vineyard which I have expressed more than once. It was always a wonderful time. Until!

Before we move on, my summary for Phase II in our lives was the longest phase. Remember Phase ll is "What You Think You Want" years. In my life it was a total of 30 years. Thirty years of soul searching to realize that I had exactly what I wanted. Life had become comfortable, satisfying, and happy. Things were about to change and I learned what the phrase, "in a minute life can turn on a dime" meant.

CHAPTER SEVEN

Phase Three: Learning to Mature

LIFE CHANGES IN AN INSTANT

It was the morning of August 25, 2006 and we were spending time on Martha's Vineyard when our lives changed forever.

Watching Nancy collapse was shocking. I had no idea what was happening, it all seemed surreal. When we arrived at the hospital, she was unconscious. We were told she experienced a brain aneurysm. Nancy was flown to Boston Medical Center. During that time, I took Ed and Mary Ann to the ferry to get them back to New Bedford. Brian and Cathy came with me to pack up a few things along with our dogs. We had to rush down to catch the ferry back to Wood's Hole, so that I could eventually make my way to Boston.

My father and sister met me at the house where my dad would stay with the dogs. Gail drove me to Boston. I remember imagining I had a blank look on my face and experiencing no feeling in my body, numbed by this sudden turn of events. When we arrived around eleven PM, my baby was hooked up to all kinds of gadgets and was still unconscious. I was told to come back the next day to speak with the doctor. Upon returning home, I laid on top of my bed hoping it was just a nightmare.

When I woke up the next morning I was fully dressed with very little sleep. I looked beside me and there was no Nancy. My gut was in pain as I went down to the living room and collapsed on the floor curled up, sobbing uncontrollably. My dogs did not understand what was happening, I could not stop. The fear of losing Nancy consumed me. This was the first time that I felt that I had absolutely no control over anything. The amazing thing is when you are in a position like that, the body goes into shock in order to protect itself. I felt as if I was on the outside looking in. At the same time realizing I was no longer watching a movie, I was in it. The fear of the unknown and the realization of the gravity of the situation was a new world to me.

Before Gail came to bring me along with Nancy's mother to Boston, I contacted my boss Mike Longo to explain what had happened. He came by to show his support and assured me to take as much time as I needed to be with Nancy. I thank God for that kind of support.

When we arrived at her room I said " I'm here babe." She was conscious and grabbed my hand. Squeezing it tightly, I was kissing her forehead for hours. She even pointed out I was wearing the bracelet she bought for me. I was wearing it for good luck. I met with Dr. Choo, Nancy's neurologist. He shared her CAT Scan which revealed she had experienced a brain aneurysm. They were monitoring the bleeding. Nancy was alert but fighting with all the tubes she was hooked up to. She was clearly very uncomfortable.

Upon returning home that night and having the opportunity to speak with my dad, we had definite doubts about what the future held for us. The next morning, that Sunday, again I found myself crying on the floor with Slate and Tasha, all of us wondering what was going on. I gave them a ride around the fort then back to the hospital. Nancy was sedated. Dr. Choo explained that there was a possible operation that could be performed to stop the bleed. Monitoring her condition, the doctor said I must be in Boston the following morning to make a decision on procedures going forth.

In the morning, I was there with Nancy's godchild, Debbie Strong. We had to make the only decision that was left to make. Nancy was to have surgery to repair the weak blood vessel. It would take five hours or more and she only had a 50/50 chance. Do you want to talk about things moving fast and being in shock at the same time? She did make it through the surgery. I could hardly recognize her when I went to see her in the Intensive Care Unit (ICU). Nancy's head was swollen. It was a sight I will never forget. Nothing good was happening and our world was changing by the minute. I became a robot living for Nancy not knowing what I would see the following day.

The next morning we met with Dr. Choo. He explained Nancy was in a medically induced coma to help slow down the swelling in the brain. At that time, going through a sudden, shocking event, your brain only gives you what you can handle. At that moment, sorrowful thoughts and feelings were all that consumed me. I didn't dare to hope. I arrived home at the end of the day to more bad news. My dad helped me bring our dog Slate to the vet. He had to have a toe removed due to a small tumor. Needless to say, sleeping that night was not an option.

I woke up the next morning and it took only seconds to feel the tears. At that moment, the song, "If I Ever Lose This Heaven" by the Average White Band, came to mind. Well, we did lose our heaven. I knew then, I would never be the same. I knew I would never wake up with that incredible blissful feeling again. It was gone forever. Reality was peeking in its ugly head and the grieving feeling was in my gut constantly from that moment on.

Day after day, I drove to Boston Medical Center to see my baby hooked up to all those machines and in a coma. It was frustrating and depressing to see no change. I was told by one of the nurses that Nancy was "posturing" herself. I asked what that meant and she explained that Nancy was "getting ready for the big sleep." My heart sank even further. They were even cutting back her medication with the hope she would regain consciousness.

I decided at this time to write down every event in a journal to help me get an idea of where I was in this suddenly, fast changing world. I began with the day it happened and recorded everything. I was determined to stay positive. Nancy needed me more than ever. I played music on my CD player to help stimulate her brain. I talked endlessly about positive things hoping she could hear. I also had to answer the many calls which came in each night. Traveling back and forth to Boston was enormously stressful. Eating and sleeping were not on the list. It was very hard waking up each day facing the reality I may never see my baby home again. The separation was very difficult. I would kiss her pillow each night. I would do anything to survive those terrible days. I felt as if I was lost in a deep, thick forest calling for Nancy and there was no answer. It seemed like she was at the far end and I could not hear.

At that point, nine days had gone by and I was unable to listen to any music or put on the television. I was consumed in this horrible new situation. Even though the nurse told me on day ten the swelling was going down and she was breathing on her own, I still couldn't shake the fear and sadness. Everything was moving in slow motion and that was good news. I was on the outside looking in at her world. By day thirteen they took all the tubes away from Nancy's face so I could kiss her, although there was still a feeding tube.

On September eighth, the nurse stated Nancy was responding more. On that day I was pleading for Nancy to open her eyes which she actually did and grabbed my hand. I fell over her and thanked God for that great gift. I smothered her with kisses. It was the best I felt in weeks. It was time now to move Nancy to rehab for her recovery. We decided to take her to Spaulding Rehabilitation Hospital of the Cape and Islands in Sandwich, Massachusetts. It was only 45 minutes from home.

On September twelfth, Nancy was admitted to Spaulding. Now, it was a matter of maintaining care and building strength. There is a lot of rehab involved after suffering a brain aneurysm and Nancy was only given only a 1% chance of survival at the time of the event. Everyone worked hard with Nancy, I was there every day. I was told Nancy had Aphasia/Apraxia, which causes speech and muscle impairment and issues understanding language. The part of the brain that forms speech was affected during the aneurysm. That meant I would never hear Nancy's original voice again. I was devastated.

Therapy continued for the next two and a half months until we came up with a goal that Nancy would be home on November eighteenth. Two days before my birthday. During that time when I was home at night I would call Nancy so at least she could hear my voice wishing her a "good night."

On the eighty-sixth day away from home we brought Nancy home. It was a dream come true, but very different. Nancy was unable to use her left arm and needed to strengthen her legs so she could at least walk with a cane. There was a great deal of work to be done. There would be physical, occupational and speech therapy at home. I was still working and the days were long. The holidays were also different. Friends stopped by the house, so there was always someone visiting, which was appreciated. On the other hand, we didn't have any privacy which made it difficult to pull together everything that needed to be done to get used to this new life.

My priority was Nancy, but it was overwhelming.

At home care continued through the winter, however, there were insurance issues. The home therapy ended and we were tasked with finding an out-patient rehab to be able to continue with all three therapies. We chose Braintree Rehabilitation where I drove Nancy beginning March seventh, (her 60th Birthday) three times a week. It took forty-five minutes each way. It was difficult to witness Nancy's struggle trying to do simple tasks. This situation was like nothing I had ever seen or heard of before. I hadn't been through this with my parents or family members, it was an eye opener. We did continue with therapy until the insurance ran out. I learned the insurance company gauges the amount of therapy allowed based on results. Once gains are at the minimum, insurance ends. It was a very cruel way of treating families in need. When summer arrived, we had to research another facility as an outpatient alternative. Nancy needed more work with her therapies. The only good news was Nancy could move around more using her cane.

We continued to travel to Braintree until the beginning of June. Time had run out with insurance coverage. A very frustrating time because I was seeing very little progress with so much effort from both parties. The pace was exhausting. I was still working. I soon recognized the availability of people able to stay with Nancy was becoming more challenging for us. We needed to get help. The one statement that I found most frustrating was hearing, "if there is anything I can do, just ask." Then when I actually did ask there were more excuses than one could count. I am not blaming anyone, however, a sense of helplessness was creeping in. I didn't know where to turn, I had never been in the position of having absolutely no control. We were now in a position where we had to hire someone while I was working, and also find a place close to New Bedford for out-patient therapy.

What was becoming more frequent were my meltdowns. I recognized our lives had changed forever and not knowing what would come next was frightening. I felt helpless. We were able to hire a speech therapist locally. I also became acutely aware of less frequent visits from Nancy's friends. I had to figure out what we needed to do to keep her home and involved and stimulated. Life goes on for everyone, but this was not going away. On an additional note that past year we also lost my Aunt Esther, my mom's sister. Change and loss was clearly a constant in life now.

That summer, Nancy and I took our first trip to Martha's Vineyard since that terrible day eleven months ago. It was totally different because I had to do everything to assist Nancy with her care. Things were manageable, until the last night that we were there. On July 24th, Nancy and I were on the deck when she had a seizure. I called the ambulance again, for the second time in a year. It was a nightmare. The seizure was caused by after stroke symptoms and medication was needed. She remained in the hospital until the next morning. Bringing Nancy back to the cottage and packing to go home was a struggle. Nancy was totally out of it due to the medication. It took two days to get her back to where she was before the seizure. I have no idea how we got through it. Nancy's new normal rested heavily on my shoulders, my bad days could easily impact her. It was up to me to figure this out. I felt like we were on an island that was shrinking and I could only rely on myself. The realization of the total lifestyle changes we had to make was shocking. Everyone moves on with their lives. We had always had lots of friends in our circle, seeing them drift away was hurtful but inevitable. The only thing that kept me going was every morning Nancy would wake up with a smile on her face. She understood she had to adjust to her disability. She always had the strength in her character and was aware of her limitations due to the injury.

Nancy's new medication created a balance problem. She had a couple of falls but fortunately did not break anything. It became clear that I needed more help. At the time, my attitude and patience for our life was not good. I was feeling very lost and on my own. This brain injury was serious and Nancy no longer had the independence she once had.

We finally found someone from the agency to come in when I went to work. That did relieve some of the pressure on me, however, we had to pay out of our own pocket. Insurance did not cover people coming into the home. We didn't qualify for that. Outpatient therapy had stopped so we needed to keep Nancy active ourselves. We did hire someone to come in for her three therapies but there was little progress.

That summer, we were told by Nancy's friend, Ann Marie, that there was a six week program held at the University of Michigan specializing in speech therapy. Ann Marie accompanied Nancy for those six weeks. I had to stay behind because of work. It was very strange being away from her for so long, not being able to hear her voice. The stress of not knowing how she was doing was worse than if I had to take care of her.

The time passed and before I knew it she was back home. We had a new routine. I made arrangements with Lisa and her friend Maria to share the caring duties while I was at work. It also gave me some much needed down time. The constant pressure of making Nancy my number one priority was always there. It was the same routine each week with Lisa and Maria sharing the five day week. It really was a matter of survival. Slowly, I was learning the art of caregiving. The knowledge I gained gave me the understanding that it prioritized my entire day to be sure Nancy was well taken care of in addition to the challenge of taking care of myself. I was living for Nancy with no expectations from others to pitch in outside of Lisa and Maria who were working those five days. This routine continued through the winter with me having limited socialization. However, the one thing I can say at that time was that she counted on me and I knew that she loved me for taking care of her. I will always love her for the appreciation she showed to me.

During the spring of 2009, we lost Tasha. I woke up one morning to find her dead under the kitchen table. We lost our "wise ass." It was another very sad moment in the forever challenging world Nancy and I shared. Tasha's health had been declining in those last couple of months so at that time, it was only Slate who was also older at twelve years old. As far as our routine, everything remained the same. Lisa and Maria cared for Nancy by taking her to appointments, doing the shopping and simply trying to keep Nancy as comfortable and life as normal as possible.

That summer we spent a great deal of time on the backyard deck listening to music while Nancy would look at her magazines. Martha's Vineyard was not going to happen that year.

As for the following year, it was like "Groundhog Day." Everything was the same. I was not able to get together with friends, and really had no time for myself. As a result, I decided to join a gym which provided mental as well as physical benefits. During the winter months, I noticed Slate was not able to move around as well due to hip dysplasia. At that point, I was taking care of Nancy and my dog; I was always in a state of high vigilance.

We lost Slate in the spring. I had to put him down in May due to his limited mobility. It was yet another very sad loss. Slate was my buddy for twelve years. He ran with me in the park, walked with me around the neighborhood and loved to travel in the back of our SUV. It was the first time in fourteen years we did not have a dog.

During those four years caring for Nancy, I understood the ritual that was our life. From there on forward she would rely on me. I had to accept the responsibility, that I was a full-time caregiver.

CHAPTER EIGHT

Caregiving 101

As time passed on, the routine of caring for Nancy and my work was our new normal. Goals were set to help keep Nancy as independent as she could be. She was able to walk with her cane and get into a car when we went out. It was important to keep her strength up along with her happiness. Lisa and Maria continued to care for her while I was at work. My work place ultimately became more like a much needed break from my caregiving duties.

Safety played an important role. When I was not with Nancy, the thought of her safety was always on my mind. Something as simple as the phone ringing automatically made me think of her safety. Our social gatherings were limited which meant it was essentially just the two of us especially on the weekends. I found I needed as much rest as I could get when not at work. The stress of taking care of someone 24/7 took a toll on me. Joining the gym helped me deal and release the stress. It was a healthy way for me to meet new people and have somewhat of a social life.

We tried to eat out at least once a week. It gave Nancy something to look forward to. Even then, she was teaching me about who I was becoming. Not a teacher, a coach or attendance officer, but a caregiver. I had never read a book about it or spoke with anyone about caregiving. I was just getting up each morning and doing what needed to be done.

It became the last year of my career working in the school system. Thirty-five years had gone by which showed me how fast time moves on. Sadly, there was no change in Nancy's progress. She was still able to move about but the reality of our lives being so limited was frustrating. I had to think ahead of what my responsibility was going to be after retirement. When June was upon us, I thanked Maria for the time and effort she had given us over the past five years. At that point, it was all up to me. Fortunately, I learned through word of mouth two young ladies were available and willing to help. Their names were Chantelle and Britney. They split the week Monday through Friday.

The caregiving routine for Nancy had become increasingly stressful. I needed downtime because the degree of my depression was getting deeper. I was losing my identity and it was not healthy for me. Something had to give and I was grateful for the extra help given by Chantelle and Britney.

During my free time in those days, I was able to run errands, go out to eat and meet with friends. I was grateful for the mental health moment which was so desperately needed. Those moments were important for being in the right frame of mind to go home with a better attitude and stamina to complete my tasks. I found myself in a better mood with Nancy on the weekends. We enjoyed each other's company more knowing I would be allowed to get a little sense of independence. If I wasn't healthy, I couldn't be there for her. It was important for me to consider my own self care and at the same time not to disrupt caring for Nancy.

Chantelle and Britney were able to take Nancy for appointments and we lived a semi-normal life. We were able to get through my first year of retirement without any major events. We both understood how important it was for us to stay positive not knowing what would be ahead.

Our routine at home continued through 2013. However, there was another tough situation about to occur. My dad came down with lung congestion and had to be taken to Rhode Island Hospital for tests. They needed to see if any cancer was present. His mobility was slowing down so it was another worry for me to endure. He was in the hospital for about a week. I used my spare time to take care of my mother and meet my sister at the hospital each day. Shortly after that my dad went to a local rehab facility to gain some of his strength back. During that time Nancy's strength was getting worse. I was worried she had come down with the flu. So, as dad was coming home Nancy was going to the doctor and immediately was ordered to be seen at the hospital. I took her to St. Anne's in Fall River where they discovered that not only did Nancy experience a stroke in the recent past, but she also had a kidney infection due to a blockage from a kidney stone which created fever and pain.

Our poor girl was in critical condition. They had to put a stent between her kidney and bladder. It was yet another nerve racking moment feeling I may lose her again. My life was miles away from the good times of the past. At that point, the only thing going through my mind was dreaming about past great moments and wondering how everything got to this point.

Nancy came out of the surgery, however was too weak to be moved until her blood pressure went down. She was in the ICU for four days in a private room for three days. At that time, I was checking in on my dad at home and traveling to the hospital during the day. After her release she was off to rehab again. She spent five weeks there to gain her strength. It was the same facility my dad had been in so I knew many of the staff. Between visits to rehab, the hospital with Nancy and visiting my dad it was more than a full time job and it gave retirement a whole new meaning. The stress level was numbing.

Eventually, I was able to take Nancy out for rides and later home for short visits. Finally, after five weeks, she returned home.

It was late spring and home therapy was again in place. Each day, Nancy worked at strengthening her legs. I admired how her attitude had not changed. I was also able to rehire Chantelle back a couple of days a week. Brittany took on additional hours at another job so it was back to me. My dad was still not doing great and helping him walk around his house was part of our daily visit. I was living a new profession as a caregiver. My job was taking care of Nancy at home and physical therapy with my dad. I only had time for myself a few times a week at this point. I spent my time at the gym which was the only place I felt some normalcy. As I look back on it now, life felt like it was taken away and a sense of survival kicked in, it was draining.

I was aware people could see the emptiness in my eyes. The good life faded away. I had absolutely nothing to look forward to. I was exhausted. On top of that the insurance only covered a certain amount of home therapy so we needed Nancy to continue at the outpatient rehab facility. We did it for love and to survive.

That next fall, my dad's health was failing. I continued to go to the house each day to walk around with him in the house. He was always alert and knowledgeable about everything. I still needed his advice. It was wearing on my mother. She was the primary caregiver at home doing everything she could to keep dad at home. We were both doing the same job in our own homes. The realization that I might lose my dad was unbearable on top of my ongoing concern for Nancy.

I made sure Nancy and I went out for coffee each morning. It gave us a chance to be as normal as possible, including listening to soul town music, which she really enjoyed. Praying that this routine would continue was futile, for in November, my dad was rushed to the hospital. He was supposed to come home on the fourteenth, however, instead, he went to his real home, heaven. He passed away that day. It was strange when my sister came by that morning to give me the news. I thought, "good for you dad, you went home." I loved him so much. He gave me support as a child, I could not have had a better father. He was my hero. I lost the most important person in the world that day and his passing left my mother on her own. My world just kept on changing for the worse. I seemed to always expect bad news, I was getting used to disappointment. I later learned that the feelings I had were part of anticipatory grief which causes fear and depression in the time before a loved one passes or while someone is going through a major health crisis.

 The holiday season was subdued. Chantelle was still helping on Wednesday's and Nancy was living each day the best she could. We were lucky enough to watch the New England Patriots win their 4th Super Bowl. Nancy and I enjoyed watching them on Sundays, which was a major part of our entertainment. She clearly enjoyed watching me scream at the television as if I was coaching. We clung to those small moments of fun, the remnants of a former life.

 That spring we decided to adopt another dog. His name was Boone, a beautiful boy. He was a two year old mix of black Lab and hound. He had a great temperament and he was protective of Nancy. She definitely loved having Boone around and he was a boost to our lives, especially for me. We enjoyed our walks in the morning and during the summer we would spend time in our back yard with Boone making the best of what we had.

At that time Nancy was under the watchful eye of her urologist who was keeping tabs on her kidneys as it was a big concern. I was aware the odds of improvement and good health were not very optimistic. Goals were simplified but it was important to keep Nancy active. For me, it was a matter of keeping my sanity and not losing focus. I found myself worrying more about her health and losing my sense of living life to the fullest. There was no time for that.

As the fall of 2016 approached, it seemed that my worries increased. I kept in mind my life with no worries was over. Chantelle was someone I could count on for Wednesday coverage. At the same time, I was also aware of Nancy's declining health, her physical strength weakened, but her spirit was still strong. My mother was still at home but I could tell she was becoming forgetful. At this point she was in her late eighties. It was the beginning of her oncoming dementia.

Do you remember my friend Clarence Brooks? My friend who coached in the NFL? He passed away that November. Nancy and I were devastated. I became numb from losing so many family members and close friends. Being a caregiver, one does not have time to grieve. No matter what happens, the daily routine remains the same.

Clarence was coaching the Baltimore Ravens. The team of coaches came to the wake and funeral. He was well respected throughout the NFL. The team, for the remainder of the season, had a CB on their helmets. His coaching history in the NFL was remarkable. He began coaching the Chicago Bears in 1993 and moved on to the Cleveland Browns in 1999. From there, he went on to coach the Miami Dolphins the very next year. He finally ended up with the Baltimore Ravens in 2005 and coached all the way to his final days. I will always miss his Saturday night calls before each game on Sunday. I miss his friendship and kindness. I have to say there are tears in my eyes every time I think of him.

The rest of that year was not the best, Chantelle was the only person until Lucy came along. Nancy loved her as she was a very funny person. She had done this work professionally for years so it was easy to trust her. She made life easier. Life seemed to have developed a revolving door now. Trying to find good caregivers that you can trust to leave your loved one with and be able to count on is harder than you think. At the moment, it was okay.

I needed to do something to help keep my sanity, so that fall, I, along with my old friend Sue Dexter from high school decided to take dance lessons together. Sue was our massage therapist. Her husband didn't care for dancing and Nancy was unable, so we took classes in Plymouth. I looked forward to those Wednesdays. They were very different as they taught us the tango and swing. It was so much fun. Between dancing and the gym, I had social time. Thank you so much Ginger for making me feel like Fred.

My mother was beginning to forget things so Gail and I decided she needed to go to assisted living. That December, mom was moved to a place in the city. It was very nice and we felt she was safe. It was the end of an era on Weaver Street. Gail took charge of cleaning out the house while I continued with Nancy's care. That spring Lucy had an illness and was unable to work. She is fine now, however, she could no longer work with Nancy. Since losing Lucy, it was just Chantelle, and Nancy needed more help getting around.

Nancy was losing weight and her appetite was off. It was obvious she was becoming weaker. At this point it was up to me to assist her from one place to the other, she had lost a lot of her mobility. I was very stressed and concerned that I couldn't keep up with the care that Nancy needed. There was no more use for the cane. By the fall of 2018 it had been twelve years of caregiving and it was clear I was in a place I was not getting out of anytime soon. I had become a robot with no emotion and totally forgetting who I was. Every morning I woke up feeling miserable, I was sad, and mad, full of emotions. It had been so long since Nancy and I woke up happy to be alive, to be able to have a conversation, and look forward to the day. It was a dead feeling inside my soul with no expiration date. At that point I felt no one could help us. Our world was only for us to handle and survive each day. Thank God for the love we had for each other to get through it. We started every morning going to the Sunrise Bakery drive through in Dartmouth for our coffee and Boone's biscuit. It was the most normal part of the day which made us happy. Music was playing and Nancy would sing along. The part of the brain that remembered music still functioned and some lyrics were recalled. It was priceless and so sad at the same time.

On my 64th birthday that fall, it just so happened Chantelle was there for Nancy that day. I wanted to do something very different. Since I was in my own miserable world I went to a local bar and restaurant close by. It is called Joe's Original. When I walked in there, there was only one seat left at the bar, so I asked the gentlemen if the seat was taken. He turned out to be my old friend David Marshall. We went to elementary through high school together. He lived in our neighborhood when we were kids. It was a great reunion. The bartender, Tiffany, turned out to be a former student of mine when I taught at Keith Junior High School. I was happy that I connected with these two people, I felt lighter going home that night. It became a regular hump day escape for me and I started to look forward to Wednesdays. It gave me a mental lift and the stamina to go home with a second wind. I began to meet new friends. When living the life of a full time caregiver, this was a welcome break. I met another bartender, who I named "baby girl." Her name is Tiffany also. We adopted each other as dad and daughter. We currently enjoy a very special relationship. I was enjoying this change in my life. However, when it was time to go home, I had to change gears to be the caregiver I was.

I continued to go to the gym and to Joe's on Wednesday. I could not continue to drive to Plymouth for dance lessons. I needed to be available to help Nancy move around the house. She only trusted me so it was important I was close by. Joe's Original took the place of dance lessons. It was closer to home. Nancy and I continued to enjoy our Sundays watching the New England Patriots. They won yet another Super Bowl, it was their sixth. It brought pleasure into our home watching them play. I thank God for the New England Patriots!

That spring we had another set back. Nancy experienced a blockage in her colon. We once again we were back to the local hospital for a colonoscopy along with monitoring her kidneys. We never knew what to expect. The constant hospital visits, waiting rooms, procedures, explanations, phone calls, emails were overwhelming while becoming all too familiar.

After spending three days in the hospital Nancy was back home for the summer. We spent most of our time on our back yard deck. She enjoyed being out there looking at her magazines with the music playing. Keeping Nancy safe was my number one priority. The pecking order was Nancy, Boone, then me when it came to focus and attention. Boone was wonderful. He gave Nancy support when I was not around. Thankfully, the following fall of 2019 we finally were able to get extra help by hiring Maria and Fatima in addition to Chantelle's help so at that point I was covered on Monday, Wednesday and Thursday. It was helpful to free up my time to go to the gym and socialize with my new friends at Joe's Original. I also had our upstairs bathroom renovated which was helpful for Nancy not having to go too far for a shower.

In November, Nancy suffered another mini-stroke and spent three days at the local hospital. At that time there were continued complications however, we were able to have her home and continued our routine. At this time, I started to feel like I was in a one on one confrontation with the grim reaper. It was obvious that Nancy was struggling as well.

Around this time, another social gathering was started with the "boys of fall." A few of the former New Bedford High School football players from the late 1960's and early 1970's would get together every two months. It still happens today. Mike Shea organized these gatherings. I was grateful to have something to look forward to. We figured life was passing us by and it became important to see each other now and then for a good time. The holidays that year were small with Nancy, Gail, mom and me.

Trying to be optimistic, I remember texting a friend saying that 2020 was going to be a special year. I got up on February twentieth to walk Boone, and on my way out said to Nancy, "see you when I get back." Little did I know those were the last words that I would speak to Nancy. When I got back, she was on the floor. She was taken to the hospital by ambulance. I was told she had experienced another brain aneurysm. Nancy was given five hours to possibly four days to live. My heart was breaking, knowing the reality of the end was near while flashing back to all we went through in 31 years together. I was told my caregiving days were over. That statement was one I had never heard, however, I will always remember it. I was losing the love of my life.

Recently, on January 12, 2022, I had a conversation with Chantelle. She shared a very touching memory she had the last time she was with Nancy. Chantelle was caring for her when Nancy pleaded with her to dance. With Chantelle's help they danced. This was the night before she collapsed. While they were dancing Nancy was laughing and enjoying her very last earthly dance. I believe she was ready to dance and laugh in heaven. I wish I had had that impression on our last evening together at home.

Seven days later Nancy passed away. It was now the worst week of my life. I had lost my precious gift who came to me in 1989. The thirteen and a half years of caregiving were over. In retrospect, it is really something to go through the shock of losing my love and realizing I would never be with that person ever again. I remember coming home that day and hearing her laugh as if to say "I am feeling the best I have felt in thirteen and a half years. I am fine baby, now I am worried about you."

I made the funeral arrangements along with Gail and Chantelle. The three of us stood by on behalf of Nancy. The wake was only one hour. At least 100 people attended. Nancy was well loved.

I presented the Eulogy. It went like this:

> "When Nancy and I started our journey together, it was Flag Day 1989. We started to develop a team of two. Her wish for me was whatever you want and I will help. Her strength and will were limitless. She was always self-confident. She had an outstanding sense of humor and we all loved her laughter. She was the smartest person I knew. She was so beautiful on the inside and

out. She was a very giving person. Once we became a team, she gave me the strength to deal with any problem with total support. She showed me her cooking skills because she was a great cook and knew how to throw a party, as well as maintain the home. She was accountable in the relationship. My baby was always dressed to the nines and taught me how to put together an outfit. She would wake up every morning with a smile on her face. We were living in "La Vida Loca."

When tragedy struck on August 25, 2006 at 1:48 pm at Nancy's Restaurant in Oak Bluffs, Martha's Vineyard, the second part of our journey began. Nancy only had 1% chance of survival. I was told she would never wake up again. She defied the odds to teach me about humility and compassion for the one you love. The journey was long, thirteen and a half years with many glitches along the way, but she kept that beautiful smile.

The last two years were challenging. Things were very stressful, but our team kept persevering and even when the end was near, Nancy fought to the bitter end. Two important goals were accomplished with our team throughout this journey. One, Nancy taught me how to be a man, for me to understand the man I am and two, she never spent a day in a nursing home. Baby, I will live the rest of my life honoring you. I love you Nancy.

Nancy's final resting place is in the Rural Cemetery where she was buried on March 4, 2020. I will be alongside her when my time comes. My parents will be 73 paces from our plot and my dear friend Clarence is only 43 paces away. I guess we will always be neighbors in this world. Rural Cemetery - my backyard.

CHAPTER NINE

Phase Four: Learning from Grief

WAKING UP THE DAY AFTER THE FUNERAL ON MARCH 4, 2020 was by far the strangest feeling I had ever experienced. When you are used to waking with your loved one by your side for half of your life the reality of not having that anymore is heartbreaking. I look back at how I felt during that time and the only word I can come up with is numbness. I felt totally lost and alone. The house became even more quiet. I would not even turn on the television or music. My usual trips to get coffee in the morning went away. Everything I did with Nancy simply stopped. When you lose the love of your life, your body seems to have a defense mechanism which helps you cope with grief. In hindsight, I was in shock. For me, it was a great deal of silence and tears. I missed her so much I would carry on a conversation to plead with her to help me get through this difficult time.

You have to remember I always counted on Nancy. Now I was asking her to help me from the other side. My friends would reach out, however, after the phone calls I would just fall back into a deep grieving mode. Eating was difficult and I lost weight. I was in search of finding something that would help me make sense of this horrible event.

I remember the following Saturday morning as I walked Boone I began to cry and moan about losing her. I was thinking back of how long our battle lasted and about how our future plans were gone. As I continued to walk that gut wrenching feeling was deep inside my soul. I could not figure out why my breakdown was so severe. Then, at that very moment I realized it was Nancy's birthday, March seventh. It was the first time in thirty one years we were separated. That feeling was the reality of losing someone so close, and now, needing to anticipate the future milestones to come as one person, alone. I reached out to my friends Lenny and

Debbie and visited their home that afternoon for some relief. It became a new way to cope with reality to spend time with friends. I like to call it a distraction, as it does not take the pain away but talking with someone eases it. I had to find a way to deal with this thing called grief.

In the meantime, my mother, who did not know of Nancy's passing due to her dementia, was being transferred to another assisted living facility for better safety. It is fair to say my world had again changed completely, It became yet another world with new lessons to be learned. I had been a caretaker for thirteen and a half years and now it was over. I asked myself, how do I live my life now? Then, to add insult to injury another terrible event occurred just ten days after Nancy was buried. It was Covid 19. The whole world, literally, shut down because of this pandemic on March 16th. It was like a perfect storm. I was grieving and now the whole world is dealing with a pandemic. I became a different kind of robot. My routine was to wake up, walk Boone twice a day and maybe watch a movie then go to bed.

One day, while walking Boone in the park I met a new friend, Wendy Gonsalves. We had seen each other before while walking our dogs. After I told her my story we became walking dog buddies, once a week. During the pandemic, I discovered that more people had dogs than at any time. My old friend from the past, Brian Baptiste also came back into my life from those park visits.

I found myself with quite a bit of free time. There was much to be done in terms of paperwork. I had attorney visits, bank accounts to deal with and property insurance issues, you name it I had to deal with it. It took about a year for everything to be finalized. I also wanted to get a gravestone for both Nancy and me which took quite a while.

To deal with my grief, I sought out an Interfaith Chaplain, Lori Howes from Southcoast Health VNA, who was fantastic. I also purchased books specifically addressing how to deal or work with grief. During the pandemic Lori and I could only speak over the telephone. We actually never met face to face. I was also deprived of my new and old friends from Joe's. Everyone was shut off from each other. I learned quite a bit during this time. For me, the most important thing was I realized grief is like a fingerprint. Everyone grieves differently. For me, when it was time to cry, I would cry. Grief comes in waves, meaning, I would hear a song or have a memory of us together which would bring me to my knees. I also learned big decisions should not be made for at least a year. I had no plans of leaving our home as there were too many memories and I did not have the energy to move anyway.

By May, the gravestone was put in. Both Nancy and my name are chiseled on it in granite. I find it fitting we will be buried together in my former back yard where I played with the neighborhood kids. Above our names it reads "Our love for each other will last forever and beyond." Nancy was my soulmate. It makes sense to me that we knew each other before and will be back together again. She knows how much I love her.

Other friends popped up along the way, Darlene, my workout buddy and Barbara who became my meals on wheels. These people, some strangers, who I didn't know for very long helped me jump start my new life. I understood it was going to take time for me to do what was needed to work through the grief of losing Nancy and honoring my family.

During that summer, places were beginning to re-open, slowly. I decorated my backyard like every year and spent time alone there. I was happy to see my friends again at Joe's Original. It was a strange feeling to go out again not having to be concerned with caregiving and all that it encompassed. I did have Boone of course. I was reading every day, however, I was not all that comfortable going out. It was as if I was experiencing Post Traumatic Stress Disorder (PTSD). There were so many changes and the pandemic hit us all. It was overwhelming to say the least.

I continued during the fall months to write inspirational notes. It was a way for me to deal with the tremendous grief I was carrying. It was my way to survive each day trying to learn some answers or truths to questions like why we are born, why we are here and what happens after death. Sorting out the deaths of family and friends, the sorrow and pain that followed whenever I lost someone weighed heavily in my mind. Learning how to cope with this terrible feeling is a lesson I am still learning. The pandemic was still at the forefront at this time so I was limited with the amount of help I could receive. I was still in contact with my bereavement counselor, Lori, but was still working on how to decide what path to take on my new journey without Nancy. Boone was by my side and he kept me in a routine. I began to cook more by experimenting with different recipes. It was just me now.

I found myself opening my heart more. I continued looking for signs from the other side. I became more aware there was something or someone guiding me. I began to look forward to seeing friends at Joe's as they made me feel welcome and put some normalcy in the day even though I was still experiencing the deep loss of Nancy. I appreciated seeing baby girl, she was a good part of the support system in my life at this time. It is interesting how a major event can change the course of a life. Even during the holidays when Gail and I were together, it was simply not the same. The family gatherings are gone now. I do continue to decorate Nancy's and dad's grave as well as put candles around the house with the hope to see signs from above. Grief is like a shovel. It digs deep into your soul and when the hole is finished you have to find a way to breathe.

On January 6, 2021, which I call epiphany day, was also the same day our Capital was attacked in Washington, DC. What I witnessed was an attack on our democracy brought on by false information about the election. That night, my sister and I went to see Maureen Hancock who is a talented and popular spiritual medium. I was focused on finding the truth about why we are here and why we die. I have always counted on God, Jesus and my spiritual guides to help me through the most difficult times of grieving our loved ones. I received wonderful messages encouraging me to live the rest of my life honoring my family and Nancy. I experienced a great feeling which I embraced as believing their souls were with God. They were doing fine and we should rejoice in the lives they lived. This experience encouraged me to write this book. This is my way of dealing with my grief.

I wanted to work on getting my identity back living without Nancy. I continued to heal and made adjustments as needed amid the waves of sorrow which crushed me as the first year anniversary of her death approached. The week of February twentieth through the twenty-seventh was excruciating. I honored her with a one year anniversary memorial in the newspaper. It read: "Our journey started in 1989. I met my soulmate, who became the love of my life and best friend. You were the most caring partner and I was blessed you chose me to walk side by side to deal with life's lessons. You were the woman with the kind of spirit and strength of character inside, just as beautiful as you were outside. You taught me how to be a man and know what love really is. We fought the great fight together, and in the end, you needed a hero, so you became one. I am so grateful to have had you in my life, baby. Our love for each other will last forever and beyond. Love you always, Michael."

During this first year without Nancy I had the desire to connect with her by opening up to the spiritual world which looked very different to me. I began to feel Nancy's presence everywhere. In every moment, the awareness of me being guided in some way was mind blowing. From the readings I understood we are all here for a certain purpose. I learned more about God and Jesus having everything under control. Our souls need to grow. It was like learning a lesson in earth's classroom, we must provide leadership and service to humanity. Over time, I have come to understand learning by reading and listening to others who have a story to tell. My spiritual guides are a blessing however, opening up my heart for signs from heaven feels larger. By opening my heart, the knowledge gained is worth everything and even more important to listen closely to my heart. I am certain Nancy is still teaching me from the other side. I feel my dad and Nancy are guiding me while I write this book. I have learned by opening my heart I experience less pressure on myself as a human being. My love for Nancy continues to grow and I believe it will be forever and beyond.

My belief is that when you can help someone in need, there is nothing more valuable for the growth of your soul than that. This action has helped me heal through my time of grief. Since I had never been in this position before, I knew I must get up each day to cope with what life has to offer which is key. As Bishop T.D Jakes said, "one door closes and another door opens." It is important to have faith and patience. I learned life has much to offer and it is important to take advantage of and appreciate the good times we have.

As far as caregiving goes, I did not think or even know I had it in me to have done this without an instruction manual. Our love made us strong enough to handle such a tragic event. Caregiving for another human being or your loved one is the most underrated duty. Particularly, a loved one, the caregiver gives up their world to prioritize the other person as number one. Being aware of my own journey, I would pick up little statements that were meaningful to me. One statement, I recall, but uncertain where I got it, sticks with me. It is "I have been working in the mud, but would like to be up to your clouds." What this said to me was that I felt at the time that my job caregiving, although not easy, still left me open to a better, happier, future. However, when in the mix it seems impossible to see beyond the mud.

My understanding now is, I need to become a leader in the service of humanity to honor Nancy and my family's legacy. I have become more spiritual as a result of this experience and will make it a priority in my life. I learned this life is just a small part of the larger picture. I believe I will be reunited with my loved ones when my job here is done.

When I reflect upon our journey, I realize the strength we had as a couple was rooted in love from the very beginning. The love became a protective love after her first episode, so she would be safe at home. It became a different kind of love from what we had before which was already strong. Let's face it, we were in this relationship for thirty one years, nearly half my life. It was seventeen years of bliss then thirteen and a half of survival mode. I am convinced God kept us strong through those challenging years. I now know we were being guided so Nancy would have a safe landing in heaven.

I thank Nancy for the inspiration to give of myself and to be there to help her in every way. I believe I have the character to be of service to the people I love. In the end, she was and will always be my hero, just like my dad. When I think of her, a beautiful memory will come through. I smile and experience tears. This is a life where grief is a continuous reminder that every day is precious. I feel her smiling at me making sure I am doing well.

I will live the rest of my life honoring her, to make her proud and complete my journey with perseverance. It is my belief that losing someone so close is the most difficult emotion a human can go through. For me, grief counseling with Lori helped. I did not hold back the tears. I am grateful for the support from the many friends I have and I thank God.

I find it helpful to speak to God and my spirit guides. I feel them around me all the time which I take much comfort in as I do not feel alone. I am not ashamed to ask my guides for help from time to time. It helps me tremendously. They are definitely listening, no fooling. I have learned how to cope each day with my new self. Praying to God's light gives me the strength to live another day with grief, but with gratitude for the life I have now. I make an effort to begin my day with a smile on my face knowing there are beautiful people out there in the world. I believe kindness is the most valuable gift you can give to another person. I spend time speaking to Nancy which always brings me a sense of security knowing she is right there with me. As the famous Muhammad Ali said "Service to others pays rent for your room in heaven." I find it very profound.

A year after Nancy passed there were many good surprises. I would be remiss if I did not include my adopted family at Joe's Original. Everyone I encountered has been so supportive. From the start, they were welcoming every time I walked in. It is that kind of place. First, it began with the managers Norman L'Heureux, Julia Perkins, Alan Frazier and Douglas Lopes who I had the pleasure of getting to know over time. They had a genuine kind interest in my wellbeing. The girls behind the bar, such as Tiffany, "baby girl", I consider it a great gift from Nancy that we are so close. I still call her baby girl and she still calls me dad. I consider it an honor and a privilege since I did not have any children of my own. I am grateful to be gifted with a lovely young woman to treat like my own daughter. I love her dearly. And then there is Tiffany, my former student at Keith Junior High School. I can't leave out Olga Lakizo, Liz, Kate, Willow, Anna, and Brianna, they all work very hard each day. It has been a pleasure for me to witness how hard these ladies work to strive to be successful in whatever they do outside of work whether it be continuing their education or taking care of their families. It is all very impressive. I have the utmost respect for all who work there. A shout out to a few good friends I met at Joe's Original include Jim and Jayne Varao, Dave Marshall who was a classmate from way back. Dave and Ali Lagesse, Wayne and Fran always offered a good story and laugh. I also cannot forget my other new friend, Ursula. She was a good listener and we shared similar stories. They should be proud to know what an impact they had on my life moving through grief and the continued kindness they show me. We formed a small family based on mutual respect and kindness for each other. We care for each other and support happiness and success.. It was humbling. They played a huge part in helping me work through my grief. They made it easy for me to cope each day knowing they were there. It was such an unexpected and welcome surprise. I appreciate the kindness and gentle support given by everyone I encountered. I thank everyone for looking out for me during such a dark time. You were the light.

Through this time of grief, I rediscovered my true self not only for Nancy but for all the friends and family I cherished who passed away over the years. I truly believe there is a change in me from my earlier years. I believe opening my heart encouraged the many gifts I received. It is the simple surprises which continue to add value to my life. It does not matter if they are good or bad, there is always a lesson to learn. Again, in my reflection of wondering why I am here, what would be my role in Earth's class? Would I be a coach, teacher, family man or role model? I became all of those. The lesson I hold dearest from Nancy is when you love someone or something, do it with your whole heart and soul. In my case, it was Nancy, then family and friends. She was number one. I follow this simple creed of bringing compassion, love and making an effort to be kind to everyone. I go to bed each evening and reflect upon the day with the knowledge I did not upset or make someone sad by my actions or maybe even taught or touched someone who needed me in that moment. Living this way brings me closer to heaven and to God.

Being in the Fourth Phase of my life gives me the confidence to wake up each morning with the intention to make people happy. It is a much better way to live life this way versus living in anger. My days have become more peaceful. I know I still have much to learn however the knowledge I have gained keeps me grounded. I want to do the right thing, like my dad did. I am getting closer to living the life he would have wanted me to.

The answer to my change is based on the fact I stayed with Nancy to the end. Our life together, as I said before, was rooted in love and trust which was the foundation to carry us through. Being a caregiver is a very special job. Every caregiver has a similar story although with different circumstances. In my case, listing the duties for each day was important. I needed to know what the agenda was. Planning ahead made me comfortable and able to get through each day.

Here in Earth's class each individual has the opportunity to choose their own path to learn about life and how to grow in a way which feeds their soul. The journey we take is of free will and hopefully the right path is chosen. The common denominator is that we ultimately end up in the same place. Every individual's journey is different, filled with good and bad, by choice or by circumstance. The choices we make help to define who we are and will ultimately bring us to the truth.

When I talk about Earth's class, what I mean is that we are all in a classroom of life. We all learn, in different ways, how to live our life in the best way we can. Being kind to people and helping those in need are examples of how our souls can grow. What we learn benefits us in the future. Yes, mistakes will be made however, learning and understanding the pitfalls from those mistakes will help us to avoid those mistakes again and move us closer to God. Treating people with respect gives us a greater gift of love. In my mind that is the key to life. Having love in our heart makes life so much easier even during times of grief. Nancy taught me that. It takes great courage to love someone unconditionally and to know love is the greatest gift of all.

This brings me to the title of my book, "Don't Take It For Granted, The Journey Within." I understand this title can mean different things to different people. In my case, IT was the love from my family, friends and Nancy. Our life was good. I had all my loved ones around. In my mind I never thought the end would come by losing those close to me at unannounced times. I lost more people over the years than the folks I know now. Life has changed dramatically, however, I know the love I received was a gift I will cherish until class is over. IT became more powerful in the fourth phase of my life. Remembering from the beginning, if we are lucky to reach the fourth phase of our lives. If we are lucky, we learn about maturity, to actually embrace maturity, and to do the right thing for humanity.

I have become more aware of my purpose on this earth in helping to make people happy, helping people in need and teaching others by quiet example. There is a song by the Jackson Five that came out in the 1970's called "Let Me Show You The Way To Go." I loved the song back then however, now, I appreciate the message even more. Back in the day, I loved the rhythm and singing but never listened to the lyrics. The meaning of the song now is very clear, in that, it is important to continue to spread love and appreciate the love you have and enjoy all around you in life.

The reason for writing this book is to honor those who were a great influence in my life by showing me love, teaching me right from wrong and learning the difference between good and evil. Perhaps through sharing my life reflection, someone will take away the understanding that they are not alone. We all need help in different ways. Writing these words has helped me realize the wonderful life I have lived so far. I have been blessed by the wonderful people who have entered my life and who continue to help me in this fourth phase. Making the right decision may not actually be the right decision even when you think you have the answer. Life has a way of saying, "Hold up, not so fast."

During the fourth phase, my plan is simple, which is to love those who cross my path each day. It is to hold the people who have left this Earth close to my heart. I consider this a gift and a privilege to make someone's day by not taking anything for granted.

A final example of not taking anything for granted was while I was finishing this book. My best friend, Boone, my four legged friend, who had carried me each day after the passing of Nancy, passed on August 28, 2021. There were issues with his heart. I took him to the vet after noticing fluid building up in his body. The very next day Boone was euthanized. I could not put my four legged hero through any more pain. This event made me realize my world had changed, yet again. For the first time, I was truly alone after being with Nancy for thirty one years and Boone for over five. He took care of Nancy and then me, his job was done. It was time for him to leave earth and be with Nancy in heaven. My responsibilities of taking care of another living soul at home ceased. Nancy and Boone made a great team called "Love". It was a gift to be in their presence. The future holds promise with more lessons to learn. I would like to thank my old friend Joanne McQuilkin for being there for me when Boone passed. It was very important to have a dear friend to help me through such a difficult time. She came back into my life at a critical time after experiencing grief due to an unimaginable tragic loss of her own. Her support and love meant a great deal and still does. Her Boston Terrier, Hudson, has also provided me with some of the love that I missed after losing Boone.

    In closing, I am humbled and honored that you, the reader, took time to read my book. I do not consider myself a writer, but rather someone who had the desire to work through my grief differently and to share what I learned with the hope another would relate and have something to take away from my experience. I was compelled to examine my life to understand the greater things presented over time. I appreciate the richness of my relationships and accept the mistakes with no judgement. I feel the need to state it was the people mentioned in this book who had the most impact on my journey. I would like to share a quote I heard in a movie that I believe was from Mark Twain, "The two most important days of your life are the day you are born and the day you found out why." For me, when I feel like I am not a winner, time will continue to give me the opportunity to become one. The path I am on today came from all the positive influences which gave me the strength and independence to continue to move forward. My advice would be, when you experience a certain strength inside for a moment, plan a project or event to distract you from the pain. There is no pain killer for grief, only fond memories to stay above the waves.

    With these words, I feel love from Nancy every day. She was my greatest and richest gift of all. It is my prayer you take ideas, or thoughts away with you into your own life which you find to be helpful. In the meantime, I will continue to learn as life is meant for learning, so our souls grow and go on forever. It is my belief, when we see our loved ones again we will feel complete joy, relief and gratefulness to have experienced the greatest gift of all, LOVE.

    Class dismissed.

ACKNOWLEDGEMENTS

THE IDEA FOR THIS BOOK CAME AS AN EPIPHANY WHICH happened to occur on January 6, 2021. It was the same day our Capitol Building was stormed by domestic terrorists with the intention to destroy democracy. It was on that very day Gail and I paid a visit to Maureen Hancock. She shared that writing a book would possibly help me and others with their grief. Based upon what I learned, I decided to pursue this project. I got down to business doing research and eventually sat down to get to work.

I continue to be grateful for the great deal of support and encouragement from many people along the way who I feel compelled to thank formally. It has been through their love and support which made this book possible.

I have made mistakes I am not proud of, however, I continue to learn from those mistakes. Some of which included events and people not mentioned as I prefer not to give oxygen to negative thoughts. Having said that, I also learned lessons from them too. For me, this became a spiritual journey with the knowledge that no matter what happens, I am capable of making changes, as long as I am willing to do the work.

First, I would like to thank my Editor, Sarah Wreszin for coming into my life at what seemed the perfect time to assist me in writing such a personal journey. With Sarah's help, she made it easy for me to make my dream a reality by answering her thoughtful questions, her encouragement to dig deeper, sometimes uncomfortably so. It was that deep reflection which helped produce this body of work. I was able to reflect upon the past years loving and taking care of Nancy as well as others who I lost over time with gratitude and love. Thank you, Sarah. Friends forever.

I thank Maureen Hancock for her inspiration to pursue my journey. Her encouragement ultimately helped me to understand I was absolutely able to accomplish the goal of writing a book about the grief I experienced. Her spiritual reading gave me hope to understand that hate or anger is not the answer and that doing something good to help others is a far better plan.

Gail, a very personal heartfelt thank you for being there for me when I needed help with Nancy. You will always remain in my heart - a true warrior. During my time caring for Nancy, then grieving for her, you took it upon yourself to care for our mother's needs. I am forever indebted to you. It is my belief, because of who you are and how you live your life, life will be kind to you. I encourage you to continue to live every moment to the fullest with retirement coming soon. I love you, Sis.

To my dear childhood friend, Lynn Donohue DiPetta (Davidian) who was always in my corner when the chips were down and would check in on me during those difficult times caring for Nancy. Lynn was there to help out whenever she could. I consider her to be one of my greatest friends and thank her whole heartedly for inspiring me to live my life the best way I can.

To Brian Rounseville, my old college friend and "book end" during our football days at Springfield College. Our friendship spans our whole adult life. I am grateful for your support. You have always been there for me MIC. I thank God for having a friend like you. We have great stories to tell which always put a smile on my face. And, of course, I would like to thank Cathy, Brian's lovely wife for her continued love and support. I love you, Murph.

To Fred Gomes, thank you my long time friend for always checking in. We always have great times and conversations together, my brother since childhood.

To my long time friend Len Sylvia. You are as tight as a friend could ever be. Thank you for your continued support along with your wife Debbie (Edge). We have enjoyed many wonderful times over the years. You have made me a very rich man knowing you will always be there for me whenever I need you.

To John Amado and Mary, thank you for your support. We love you both and appreciate your friendship to the end of Nancy's life and beyond.

To John Gomes, we were children together who bonded later professionally working in the school system. You were kind in keeping me in the loop which I will always appreciate. You have also given me great support all through my journey with no judgement. Thank you for being one of my greatest friends, who always inspires me with words from God. Love you brother, we are friends until the end.

To Larry Burns, when Nancy had her stroke, you were there for me. I thank you for our conversations and support during that time, you've been a true friend.

To Chantelle Santiago, you came to us at a critical point in Nancy's caregiving when we needed you most. Your time with Nancy was a gift. Nancy and I will forever be grateful for you. We all developed a special relationship with you during the process of caring for Nancy, much like a daughter. Love you always.

To "The Boys of Fall" which was initiated when we all were mindful of the fact that we were losing close friends and family, and realized life was too short. Our Captain Mike Shea leads us to get together every two months to reminisce about our lives past and present. Thank you to Mike, Alan Zexter, Pat Walsh, Bruce Manssuer, Tom Spence, Don Girouard and all the great guys who played for New Bedford High School football teams. I appreciate our gatherings and continued support. You are living legends to me.

To Jim Roper, my main man from Detroit. I want to thank you for coming into my life at the right time. You were there for my father, Nancy and me. Nancy loved when you visited. You have been a great friend. I will never be able to repay your kindness and knowledge.

To Darlene Quail, my workout friend. It was rewarding meeting you at the gym and I will always remember our conversations and your listening ear after Nancy passed. You made my hard times easier. Thank you.

To Mathew Medeiros, my other workout partner, you will never know how much you helped me. Working out with you was a wonderful distraction from life at home. Thank you for your friendship. I wish you the very best life has to offer.

To Sue Oliveira, thank you for our occasional sit downs. I appreciated the fun we had and your great advice. Thanks, Cuz.

To Mike Longo, who was the Superintendent of New Bedford Public Schools and a good friend. When Nancy had her stroke you were able to provide the time and the space I needed to sort out what had to be done to take care of Nancy. You cannot imagine what a gift that was to me. You are indeed a dear friend.

To Judge Bettina Borders and everyone at the Juvenile District Court. I could not have performed my job duties and taken care of Nancy without your assistance. You created a work environment where I felt close to everyone.

Memories of all the fabulous people keep me going even today. Thank you, Judge.

To Ron Walsh, thank you for your friendship and support for the past twenty five years. Nancy loved seeing you and enjoyed your visits with us.

To Terri Cormier, head of the probation department, thank you for your continued support and friendship.

I would be remiss not to mention that after a long separation from my dad, my Uncle John and Dan Silveira along with Patsy, came back into our lives. It meant a great deal to my dad to be reunited before he passed. Thank you so very much.

To Barbara Perreira, thank you for the delicious meals on wheels which were and still greatly appreciated, as well as our new friendship. I am happy you came into my life.

To Buddy Rocha, I am privileged to be on your list of "old school friends." You have brought great times into my life, along with your extraordinary talent as a fabulous Cape Verdean chef. Thank you, my brother.

To Ken Soares who has a great talent to share our stories from back in the day. Thank you, brother, for the priceless memories and being a life long friend.

To my park friend, Jeanne Wiley. Our walks and talks with our dogs Molly and Boone helped me a great deal. Thank you.

To Lucy Macedo, thank you for being a ray of sunshine when you entered our home to care for Nancy. Our laughs were priceless.

To Dr. Larry Finnerty, thank you for being a great friend. Your sense of humor always had us in stitches. You kept things light.

To Billy DePina, the grown man who is raising his two sons with his wife who still calls me Coach. I love you Billy.

To Roxanne Defreitas, thank you for your continued support and friendship. Always in my corner.

I would be remiss if I did not thank some of the great people I met at Workout World Gym. You gave me a sense of normalcy during and after Nancy's passing, tough days. Thank you so very much for being there, not knowing how much you helped me: Dan Romanowicz, Ray Wills, Joey Gonsalves, Rob Belliveau, Shawntel Amado, Mark Rosofsky, David Houtman, John Turner and Mark Reedy. I look forward to seeing you at the gym. To Charlie, thank you for the 5 yen good luck coin from Japan. Your gesture meant more to me than you'll ever know.

To my neighbors, your continued support never goes unrecognized. Thank you for making me feel at home with your kindness for both Nancy and me.

I cannot go without mentioning my dear friend Joanne McQuilkin again, for reconnecting with me and our childhood from past days in school. You have been a tremendous gift sent back to me with your knowledge and experience of how life is. When you offered to help piece together my final product with hours of your expertise, this book was able to be published. I consider us friends forever and will always cherish our time getting us through our transitions in Earth's class. May you graduate this class with honors knowing you have been an angel on earth for your family, friends and me. I love you always.

Finally, Nancy was fortunate to have many female friends who kept in touch with her throughout our life changing experiences. A heartfelt thank you goes out to all of you for your support, whether it be physically or spiritually during the years prior. To name a few of some of the great teachers and friends. Karen Garcia, Donna Parker, Doreen Beneditti, Sue Abaray and Kathy Castro. And to Sandy Tillett for her friendship and special pictures.

For Bob Simmons: As I finished writing this book, another shocking event entered to remind me why life is so precious. Bob was truly one of my best friends who was there for me since 1976. We had great fun. He and his wife Karen checked in on us often and put a smile on Nancy's face. He was always there for our family. When he entered the room, smiles would appear. We will be missing one more smile to grace our lives, which we took for granted. "I love you brother" were his last words spoken, which will always be in my heart.

SPECIAL MOMENTS OF

Love and Wisdom

I WOULD LIKE TO HONOR MY PARENTS, VIRGINIA AND GUY for their unconditional love and support throughout my life as well as my sister Gail. Due to my mother's current condition of dementia one might think she is unaware of my book but I know with certainty in her soul, she knows. My mother was the silent partner who made the family happy. She actually controlled everything that went on in our home. She was my greatest fan and supporter as well as being there for my dad and sister. She ran a tight ship which ran smoothly. She did not have to say "I love you" because she showed us with every action. My mom cared for my dad until the end which took a lot out of her. I had the greatest childhood because of my parents. I understand why I miss her so much. My words will never reflect the way I care for my mom.

My mom was my greatest cheerleader on the planet. Honoring her is a privilege. She showed me love without having to say it. She wrote a diary reflecting my younger life which I recently found. It begins March 31, 1962. I was seven years old. She titled it "To my son, Michael Guy Oliveira" by Virginia Oliveira. It began with Dear Michael. The diary contains detailed events I neither knew about or have forgotten. For example, I was born at 2:08 AM, 7 pounds 4 1/2 ounces. She listed the places I grew up and the schools I attended. What makes this gift so special is the clarity she expressed about my young life events in her beautiful penmanship.

THE JOURNEY WITHIN

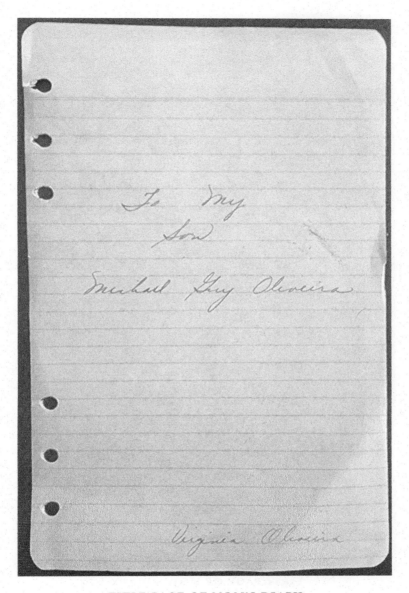

TITLE PAGE OF MOM'S DIARY

DON'T TAKE IT FOR GRANTED

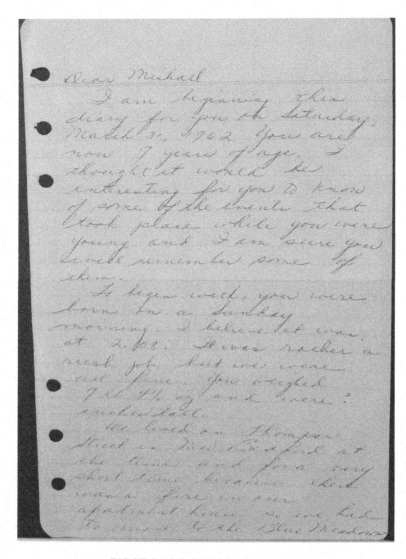

FIRST PAGE OF MOM'S DIARY

I appreciate my mother's effort keeping a diary. She took care in including the names of all the people who entered my life. She kept a watchful eye on me during the 1960's and early 1970's. I am grateful for the early knowledge of my life story. I found this book two years after Nancy's passing. Gail had given it to me a few years earlier, however, I was so involved caring for Nancy I put it aside to read at another time. As I write this book, it will be exactly sixty years at the end of this month that my mom started her diary. For me, this is the greatest gift a mother could give her son. I could hear her voice as I read her written word with tears rolling down my cheeks. She knew me better than anyone and put it in writing. I was not aware of how proud she was of all the accomplishments I had as a boy and teenager. Her love was big and I felt it. Now, because of the circumstances from her dementia, that love in my soul has grown and my love for my mother will always remind me of how well I was loved.

The last part of the diary was written during Christmas 2002. She wrote "Michael, dad and I are sure your memories are better than ours. We would not trade any of our memories for anything in the world."

One last hurdle I needed to clear before finishing this book is seeing my mother regularly at a local nursing home. It is beautiful seeing her smile and walk around the facility. She is happy, even dealing with dementia. I feel that with the climax of this project nearing, I felt it appropriate to continue spending more time with mom while she is still here knowing our love for each other is forever. I love you so very much ma. You are in my heart for eternity.

My dad was equally influential in our upbringing. He was the calm and steady rock who quietly got his point across with all the love and wisdom a man could only give his family. He was invested in his community. He created a program for the New Bedford Police Department to bring underprivileged youth to the Boston Red Sox games every summer. He and his fellow officers would provide transportation and food. It was a big deal because it is possible that many of those kids were seeing a professional game for the first time in their lives. His generosity for the community shined for many years. Now, these adults who attended those games and knew my dad back then are pleased and very appreciative to share their experiences with me. His family and the community were very important to him. Everybody loved Guy Oliveira.

Even when his health was in decline, his strength came through until the last day of his life. His strong belief in God and Jesus helped him keep his dignity to the end. He wrote down many thoughts which kept his spirits up preparing for the inevitable. An example would be "The Challenge," a creed for those who have suffered and asked for strength and good health to do better things. To pray to our merciful God and Jesus gave him not only the strength to combat his personal struggle against his illness, but to also, with courage, patience and wisdom fulfilled his life's journey.

He took time to write down the steps to handle a disturbing diagnosis. I pondered these questions as I navigated through tragedy and caregiving with Nancy.

"Do not try to get through this battle alone. Stay sane. The emotional stress of battling a serious illness can take a toll on one's mental health as well as challenge the stability of relationships. Joining a support group to vent to others who have been in similar shoes is helpful. It is important that it is an optimistic group. What good is life if it is found in solitude and loneliness? What good is life if to others happiness you cannot bring? What good is life when the heart is sad and lonely when there is no happiness at all, when there is not a smile to make life worthwhile? What good is life if there is no one to share burdens as they begin to fall when all seems lost as if there is no cause? What good is life?"

My dad always had a particular outlook on life. He put his heart and soul into everything he did. I learned everything I needed to know from him. His guidance helped me learn what I had to do as a caregiver. The best gift a father could give his son are great memories of the love that now resides in my heart. As I write this tribute, I acknowledge mom and dad were tremendously successful with how they lived their life and worked through, together, the obstacles they faced. The love they gave each other, their children and the community explains the last sentence in the book. My love for both of them runs deep and is infinite.

Just when things seemed to be going smoothly I found myself on another emotional rollercoaster on July 8, 2022. Grief peeked its evil head out again with a cruel sense of humor. I checked my phone and saw an alarming message. It said "David Marshall died today in an accident." Earlier, I mentioned running into my old childhood friend David. We would see each other from time to time and catch up on our lives. I was devastated by this news. Grief set in again that night and through part of the next morning. Tears of sorrow and disbelief entered my soul. It was yet another loss of someone special in my life. The power of grief came back with all its power from the past and the present that morning. As sorrow was in my heart, I checked the message again, and behold, there was a message sent from David's account stating, "I still have a pulse, I've been hacked." It was like he was resurrected from the dead. The feeling I had after reading that message was of great joy and relief. Not today, Reaper.

I try to wake up each morning like it is Christmas, and be open to a gift from heaven, big or small and cherish it for the rest of the day. Everything in my life has become more precious. For example, just this morning on the sixteenth year anniversary of Nancy's brain aneurysm I was resting on the couch and looked up into the sky to witness a cloud in the shape of a heart. To me that was a gift.

Finally, a tribute to the greatest teacher in my life, Nancy. We are soulmates who will meet again. I will always remember her beautiful face smiling at me. There is a wound in my heart that will never heal. However, with her spirit to guide me, I will do the work needed to be done here on Earth. I will always be the keeper of Nancy's castle as long as I live. Death be not proud because Nancy lived her life with dignity and grace and God was with her at every step of the way.

    I have been blessed with people who entered my life past and present. I consider myself a very lucky man! A song comes to mind when looking through scattered pictures: "The Way We Were."

THE WAY WE WERE

FIGA, BLANCHE, ELSIE, MY PARENTS, TONY, AND HARRY

DON'T TAKE IT FOR GRANTED

DEREK AND GAIL

GANG ON DECK

THE JOURNEY WITHIN

WITH FRIENDS AT A FUNCTION

COUSINS BOBBY, DAVID AND NICKY

DON'T TAKE IT FOR GRANTED

MAN CAVE

COACHING AT NEW BEDFORD HIGH SCHOOL

THE JOURNEY WITHIN

NANCY AT ALDEN

WITH BRIAN & BUDDY

DON'T TAKE IT FOR GRANTED

NANCY ON VINEYARD WITH SLATE AND TASHA

IN THE BEGINNING

THE JOURNEY WITHIN

DAD AND ME, BACK IN THE DAY

DON'T TAKE IT FOR GRANTED

BABYGIRL

FAMILY

THE JOURNEY WITHIN

JO AND HUDSON

WORDS FROM MICHAEL

I NEVER CONSIDERED writing a book about my experiences in life. From the days of teaching in the classroom, I kept a journal of my daily routine. It gave me a sense of comfort to recall the positive and negative points of my curriculum, as I tried to improve it each year. As my life went from the school classroom to Earth's classroom, I continued to monitor important moments, not knowing it was practice for what lay ahead. Growing up surrounded by love from my family and friends has given me the strength to live each day with hope and faith. When my beautiful Nancy suffered a serious brain aneurysm in 2006, my journals organized my thoughts, daily events and situations, not knowing it would be in a book one day. Through my experiences, there came a knowledge that there is something more than just living our lives here on earth without a purpose. My memoir describes the highs and lows, the gut wrenching pain, the isolation and the hopelessness that caregivers face. With faith and love, there can be hope for the future while living with pain and grief.

By keeping an open mind, love will help guide you to conquer your goals. My parents gave me a strong base to start life. Nancy finalized it with a deep love that allowed us to navigate a life changing event. Her strength and love supported me through my journey of learning earth's lessons and my role of becoming a caregiver for the one I loved. My life lesson is simple. With God's help, I was inspired to never take love for granted. "The most precious gift on Earth."

Hez 1.

Heal: